The Ball

Other Books by Daniel Paisner

The Ball

Mark McGwire's 70th Home Run Ball and the Marketing of the American Dream

Daniel Paisner

VIKING

Published by the Penguin Group

Penguin Putnam Inc., 375 Hudson Street,
New York, New York 10014, U.S.A.
Penguin Books Ltd, 27 Wrights Lane,
London W8 5TZ, England
Penguin Books Australia Ltd, Ringwood,
Victoria, Australia
Penguin Books Canada Ltd, 10 Alcorn Avenue,
Toronto, Ontario, Canada M4V 3B2
Penguin Books (N.Z.) Ltd, 182–190 Wairau Road,
Auckland 10, New Zealand

Penguin Books Ltd, Registered Offices:
Harmondsworth, Middlesex, England

First published in 1999 by Viking Penguin,
a member of Penguin Putnam, Inc.

1 3 5 7 9 10 8 6 4 2

Copyright © Daniel Paisner, 1999
All rights reserved

Library of Congress Cataloging-in-Publication Data

Paisner, Daniel.
The ball : Mark McGwire's 70th home run ball and the marketing of the
American dream / by Dan Paisner.
p.   cm.
ISBN 0-670-88776-5
1. Baseballs—United States—Marketing.   2. McGwire, Mark, 1963–   .
3. Home runs (Baseball)—United States.   I. Title.
GV875.2.P35   1999
796.357'64'097309049—dc21   99-26135

This book is printed on acid-free paper.♾

Printed in the United States of America
Set in ITC Officina Serif
Designed by Jaye Zimet

This book is for my father,
who took me to my first baseball
game, and then some.

"The sky was the limit, and I just found out what the sky was."

—Twenty-six-year-old research scientist Philip Ozersky, after selling Mark McGwire's 70th home run ball for over $3 million at a Madison Square Garden auction on January 12, 1999

Contents

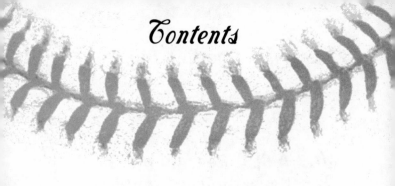

The Ball

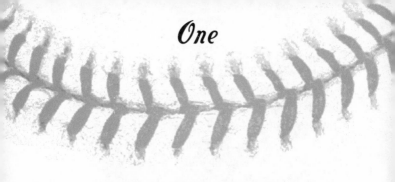

One

Pregame

*Or, Putting $3.005 Million into
Something Resembling Perspective*

We live in interesting times.

We live in a time when top high school athletes aspire to careers as professional wrestlers, when professional wrestlers aspire to be governors, when governors sign book deals before they sign their first pieces of legislation.

We live in a time when the thing to do has ceded to the *correct* thing to do, when Princeton sophomores no longer romp naked across campus courtyards on the night of the first snowfall because school administrators are concerned more with appearances than tradition and windchill factors.

We live in a time when the values we place on our culture threaten the values our culture places on us, when the protested sale of a Jasper Johns painting that has decorated New York's Lincoln Center theater lobby for thirty-five years stands in the way of as much as $15 million in needed funding.

And as long as we're on it, we live in a time when dollar bills change hands as carelessly as if they'd been printed by Milton Bradley, when the market capitalization of fledgling internet companies rivals the gross national product of, say, Belgium. When money burns the kinds of holes in our deep pockets that can't keep us from our impulses.

We up the ante at every conceivable turn, and at some inconceivable ones. The first recorded live birth of septuplets one year is topped by the first recorded live birth of octuplets the next, and in each case the makers of diapers and minivans and headache relievers claim pole position to sponsor the ordeal. For every hard-to-fathom Paula Jones, there is an even tougher to swallow Monica Lewinsky. (Forgive, please, the unfortunate image this last statement calls to mind.) Nothing is as it was. More than ever before is not nearly enough. Bigger is not only better, it's vital. Hollywood sequels must outspend, outwit and outearn the movies on which they are based. Superstar athletes leapfrog each other in the race for top salaries, while world champions are called upon to repeat and *three-peat* or risk a slow fade. New and improved has become our baseline condition. We've seen it all, but we haven't seen enough. We lose sleep over what we might miss, underneath the related worry that time will catch us napping.

Take baseball, our national game. It is no longer sufficient to simply *go* to the ballpark to root for the home team. Forget for a moment that this year's home team resembles last year's home team in uniform only and that lately it seems even the uniforms are redesigned from one season to the next. (Ah, the better to sell new hats and jerseys to the same subset of fans, year after year.) Now we must take something *back* from the ballpark as well, something tangible, with real market value. Now we need an autograph, a foul ball, a ticket stub. Even a shred of peanut shell wedged in the tread of a sneaker can yield a substantial return, if it can be proven that the corresponding nut was consumed during some memorable moment or other. The *being there* has been replaced by the *having been,* and we have made it so we must vigilantly one up each other to validate our place in the puzzle. We need the all-star's rookie card, mint, to prove our worth as fans.

Consider the 1998 baseball season. The New York Yankees, with 125 victories, were the class of the field, but their successes were filtered through a constant context, weighed against other teams, from other times. We could not appreciate the Yankees for what they were; we had only to appreciate them for what they were not. The same paradigm could be found in the summer-long assault on the vaunted home run records of seasons past. Mark McGwire, Sammy Sosa, Ken Griffey, Jr. . . . the game's marquee sluggers could not step to the plate without the shadows of Babe Ruth and Roger Maris looming larger than their own. And yet, somehow, the entire cast managed to transcend what we had once held as immutable standards, while at the other end, it was left to the fans to divvy up the spoils.

And what a lot of spoils there were to be had! There had always been a quietly viable market for baseball collectibles, but there had never been anything like *this:* commemorative bats, limited edition coins, Franklin Mint curios, collectible Wheaties boxes, stamp-signed photos and plaques, gold-foil baseball cards, crystal baseballs cut and appropriately engraved by Tiffany's. Ridiculously priced souvenir cups that had once held ridiculous amounts of flat soda. Then there was the real deal: the game-used bats and hats and gloves and cleats of the stars themselves. The undershirt worn (and, presumably, washed) by David Wells from the perfect game he pitched during a Beanie Baby Day promotion at Yankee Stadium, on May 17, along with a stadium-issued Valentino Beanie Baby, which together were sold at auction by Christie's East on November 3 (lot #264) for $862.50. The lineup card from the St. Louis Cardinals' final game of the season, consigned to the same Christie's auction by manager Tony LaRussa on behalf of his pet project, the Animal Rescue Foundation—ARF, of course—and sold to the highest bidder for $29,900.

But most of all, there were the home run balls. Never before in the history of the game had so much attention been focused on so little—and never before had there been so much of so little to go around. The balls were simple game pieces, valuable more for what they represented than for what they actually were, and as the leading home run totals mounted they came in bunches. Granted, it has always been a big deal for a fan, young or old, to actually *catch* a home run ball, no matter if it was hit off the bat of an emerging icon like Mark McGwire or a platoon catcher like Tom Lampkin. A home run ball is a home run ball is a home run ball. If you were lucky enough to make the grab yourself, the ball was priceless. As a commodity, however, the game balls were of dubious interest, except among certain denizens of the sports collectibles market—those big-bellied, vintage-team-jacketed, pinky-ringed, badly hairpieced individuals who haunted baseball card shows and autograph signings as if their lives depended on it. Their interest, in turn, carried the weight of baseball history—or, at least, the perceived weight of baseball history, as it was filtered through the collectors' own sensibilities.

If you weren't "in the hobby," it was possible not to notice all the getting and spending. That is, until 1992, when actor Charlie Sheen paid $93,500 for the baseball that somehow managed to find its way off the bat of New York Mets center fielder Mookie Wilson and through the legs of Red Sox first baseman Bill Buckner, during Game Six of the 1986 World Series. It was harder for us to look away from that kind of transaction than it was for Buckner to keep his eye on that ball. Going into the 1998 season, Sheen's Mookie ball was the standard for a game-used baseball. It was a lot of money, to be sure, but it was paid out by a movie star inured by excess and seven-figure paydays to what that kind of money represented to the rest of us. We were conditioned to that sort of math. The numbers made strange sense, especially when it was reported that Sheen's souvenir would be put on display at the All-Star Café in New York's Times Square, a restaurant in which the actor was said to have a financial interest.

It was, alas, a business expense.

And then Mark McGwire came along and changed the equation. Indeed, the most prodigious home run hitter in recent baseball history could not have struck a mightier blow for the spirit of enterprise if he had swung his bat all season long at a Fugifilm Blimp-sized piñata filled with hundred dollar bills. Even a mid-season report that McGwire was using the muscle-building nutritional supplement androstenedione did little to diminish his accomplishments, as the scramble for his record-breaking home run balls set in motion the kind of frenetic after-market more commonly associated with gold and pork belly futures than with mere souvenir. Ball hawks staked choice seats in the outfield bleachers, scarfing up tickets to late-season games in lots of two dozen or more. Field box ticket holders happily traded their now-cheap seats for a $6 dollar segment of bleacher. Memorabilia specula-tors went to ballparks carrying valises stuffed with cash, as much as $20,000 according to some reports, hoping to buy back balls on the spot. Three collectors pooled their money and offered a $1 million annuity to the fan who came up with the record-establishing home run ball, payable over ten years. News accounts polled experts to determine what these balls might be worth to collectors, or to corporate interests looking to generate tie-in busi-ness, while those in the market for them pretended to ignore the estimates. And, in a strange piece of inter-connected speculation, one fan, who received signed bats and balls from Chicago Cubs' right fielder Sammy Sosa in exchange for one of his record-territory home run balls, immediately contacted a memorabilia broker to determine what those traded-for items were worth in the hobby.

What had changed, in the off-seasons leading up to 1998, was the way collectors had siphoned the emotional value from game-related items and replaced it with mar-ket pricing. Children no longer traded baseball cards with their friends, preferring to hoard them in their original wrappings to preserve their future worth. Autographs were no longer clamored for but collected in orderly fash-ion in exchange for a signing fee. Game-used balls were no longer displayed on mantels; signed scoresheets were no longer tacked to bedroom walls. Today's collectors handled their "merch" like drug dealers, wrapping their overpaid-for items in sandwich bags and stuffing them into sock drawers or bank vaults for safe keeping. There was less percentage in actually enjoying these artifacts than there was in acquiring and maintaining them.

As the 1998 campaign took on its record shape, the talk among memorabilia dealers turned to some of the more famous home run balls that never made it to market—or to the Hall of Fame. The "shot heard 'round the world," which left the hands of Ralph Branca and the bat of Bobby Thompson, decided a pennant and was never seen again. One of the most dramatic pinch-hit home runs in World Series history, Kirk Gibson's stunning blast in Game One of the 1988 series. One of the most dramatic game-ending home runs in World Series history, Carlton Fisk's twelfth-inning deposit into the safety net of Fenway Park's "Green Monster," to win Game Six of the 1975 World Series. And perhaps the most dramatic home run of all, Bill Mazeroski's 1960 World Series winner, in the bottom of the ninth, Game Seven.

(In an everybody's doing it twist, former Cincinnatti Reds left fielder George Foster would surface during the off-season with the Fisk ball, which he had quietly held all along. "I just took it home with me," he said, in announcing plans to auction the ball during the 1999 season.)

The pages of publications like *Sports Collectors Digest* filled with profiles of such noted ball holders as Richard Arndt, the Brewers' groundskeeper who was fired in 1976 for failing to return Hank Aaron's 755th and last home run ball, and who was reportedly looking to at last put the ball up for sale, perhaps for as much as $1 million.

All of a sudden, Charlie Sheen's $93,500 was starting to look like walking-around money. And it wasn't just the balls that commanded our attention, or the meditations on their value. It was the surrounding circus, the sustained carry. That such as this took place for the most part in St. Louis—a cradle of baseball history, the home of *The Sporting News*, Rawlings Sporting Goods Company, and Anheuser-Busch, one of the game's great lubricators—only added to the melodrama. The rest of the world couldn't help but notice, while in the economically, racially, and ethnically diverse suburbs of St. Louis it sometimes seemed people could think of little else. Sweet old ladies who cared hardly at all for baseball and knew nothing of its traditions rooted for Mark McGwire. Preschool children could tell you his name. The homeless and disaffected could pick him out of a precinct lineup. On street corners, resourceful young men sold commemorative Sunday editions of the *St. Louis Post-Dispatch* for $10 apiece the same day they were put on sale, after cleaning out newsstand and convenience store racks at $1 each. We addressed each other in hypotheticals—would you keep one of the record home run balls, or sell it, or give it back?—and judged ourselves in the response.

For all its pomp and foofaraw, McGwire's historic campaign could not have come at a better time for the game. According to Roger Angell of *The New Yorker*, McGwire "saved baseball's ass" when a whole lot more of its anatomy needed saving. Team payrolls were up (a record 326 players earned more than $1 million in 1998 salaries) and team revenues down. The sport had seen an erosion in fan support dating to the strike-shortened season of 1994, and though fans had been coming back in bigger numbers since Cal Ripken trumped Lou Gehrig's storied consecutive game streak in 1995, they could not come back quickly enough. The logos atop the capped heads of America's youth had been more likely to represent teams from the National Basketball Association or National Football League, or foulmouthed cartoon characters, than they were to stand for anything remotely connected to baseball. And the pace of the game was thought to be too meandering to hold the short attention spans of a generation raised on music videos, computer games, and tag-team, full-contact bungee jumping.

Of course, it wasn't just McGwire vested with all that ass saving. It was the couple dozen other stars at various stages of what could turn out to be Hall of Fame careers: Griffey, Ripken, Maddux, Bonds, Clemens, Gwynn. . . . It was the shooting script of the developing season. It was Orlando "El Duque" Hernandez, brother of 1997 World Series Most Valuable Player Livan Hernandez, surviving a raft trip from Cuba over apocryphally shark-infested waters to anchor the Yankee pitching staff for most of the season. It was Cubs rookie Kerry Wood, striking out 20 batters in one game and looking to all comers like a seasoned ace. It was Juan Gonzalez, threatening Hack Wilson's single season record for runs batted in; Paul Molitor, putting the flourish to a thorough-going career; Dennis Eckersley, returning to Boston to see if there was anything left in his once-golden arm. It was the expansion of the game to the great southwest, and the taking root of inter-league play. It was the void left by a looming professional basketball lockout and the wistful reminiscences of baby boomers looking over their shoulders at the game of their growings-up.

Nevertheless, the staggering home run totals of Mark McGwire and Sammy Sosa were at the center of attention, and as the season drew to its close, the focus was on these two gentle giants, who took turns congratulating each other and safeguarding the spotlight. Their sights, in turn, were set on the single season home run record of 61, established by Roger Maris of the New York Yankees in 1961, a record that was once thought untouchable.

With each home run, speculation grew.

Major league officials began marking and tracking the balls pitched to McGwire and Sosa and put in place "extraction" teams to ensure fan safety.

The Baseball Hall of Fame and Museum dispatched "extraction" teams of its own to every late-season Cardinals and Cubs game, hoping to convince fans to part with their prized souvenirs in exchange for posterity and a lifetime pass to Cooperstown.

St. Louis Cardinals executives met informally to discuss whether the club should have a policy for employees who might retrieve the record balls. (It was determined that it should not, other than to wish the ball holders well, whatever they decided.)

The Internal Revenue Service offered its two cents on whether a ball caught by a fan and returned to McGwire or Sosa would carry any tax implications. (It would, or it wouldn't, depending.)

Sportswriters, with bigger and bigger news holes to fill, began calculating the cumulative distance traveled by McGwire's home runs. A game of inches was for the first time measured in miles, and at 29,598 feet McGwire's what-would-happen-if-you-laid-all-of-his-home-runs-end-to-end? target lay somewhere in the five to six mile range. Six miles! That's about half the distance from home plate at Oakland's Alameda County Coliseum, McGwire's home stadium for over ten years, to the left field stands at San Francisco's 3Com Park across the bay.

And yet for all of the excessive calculations, for all

of the anticipation and preparation, for all of the head scratching and jaw dropping and fist pumping at each new notch to the single season record, one question remained: Where would this march on baseball history ultimately end? Or, strike that, one *basic* question remained, but there were several branches to it. Who would finish out in front, Sosa or McGwire, or perhaps even Griffey in a late-season surge? Would Maris's record stand? And, if it fell, who would come up with that ultimate home run ball? What would he or she do with it? What would their tax bill look like? What would be the most valuable prize—the 61st home run, to tie the record? The 62nd, to break it? Or the one that sets the new standard? What would be its ultimate value, and to whom?

The answers, at bottom, would say a good deal about who we were—as baseball fans, and as caring, thinking animals, both—and would prove far more compelling than anything else going on in the world of sports, at the other end of the World Series.

And, for some, the most compelling piece was this: The talk would turn on one swing of the bat, one monumentally lucky fan, and one baseball.

Just one.

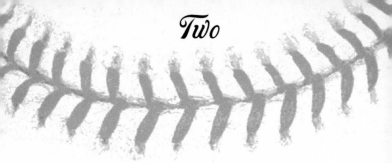

Two

Infrared, White, and Blue

*Or, How an Official
Baseball Got Its Spots*

What happens when a thing needs doing and it's never been done before?

Well, if you work in a corporate setting, chances are you take a meeting—and if you work in baseball's corporate offices, you take that meeting at the ballpark.

Such a meeting took place on Saturday, August 29, 1998, beneath the Busch Stadium stands, and the key items on the agenda were the role of Major League Baseball in authenticating the record home run balls and in providing security in the outfield seating areas. The meeting was called by Kevin Hallinan, executive director of security for Major League Baseball. Also in attendance were two members of Hallinan's staff, Ruben Puente and Linda Pantell, and several members of the Cardinals organization, including vice president of stadium operations Joe Abernathy, director of stadium operations Mike Bertani, director of security Joe Walsh, and equipment manager Buddy Bates. Serendipitously, the Cardinals were playing the Atlanta Braves at the time of the meeting, and Hallinan asked the Braves' traveling secretary Bill Acree to sit in; in 1974, Acree had been involved in the marking of the balls pitched to Henry Aaron as he approached Babe Ruth's all-time home run mark.

Hallinan thought Acree could tell them how the Braves marked the Aaron balls, but there was nothing to tell. Team officials just slapped some hand-scratched numbers on the balls and threw them out there, Acree said. Nothing fancy. Now they were talking about special technology and invisible markings. It was a whole new ballgame—which, when you work in baseball's corporate offices, is often the case.

Hallinan considered his position. To the best of anyone's recollection, the only other time game balls had been marked was during Cal Ripken's march on Lou Gehrig's consecutive game record, and that effort was handled quietly by the Baltimore Orioles. Here, Hallinan was about to pass the responsibility for marking the 1998 balls to Bates, but as he spoke to Acree he realized he'd be off-loading a tremendous responsibility on him and on the Cardinals. Right then, he realized baseball would have to take the lead on this because what they were facing was bigger than just the Cardinals. Of course, Hallinan also had the Cubs to consider, with Sosa making his own push at the record, but what he meant was that it was a bigger responsibility than any one team should have to undertake. The integrity of the game was on the line.

Before Hallinan could move to the next point on his list, the stadium began to rumble with what was happening on the field. Outside, in the real world, Mark McGwire had been tossed from the game by home plate umpire Sam Holbrook for arguing a third strike, and from the noise that reached these security officials in their small meeting area, it didn't sound as if the fans were happy about it. Immediately, Hallinan said, they switched into security mode and broke the meeting to help quiet the crowd. They had the radio on, and one of the announcers worried a riot would break out in the stands.

The incident reminded those in charge what they already knew: Security would be as much of a problem as authenticating the baseballs. To Hallinan's thinking, it was even more of a concern; the last thing he wanted was for someone to get hurt. There'd be enough cameras focused on the baseballs and the people who caught them that it was likely his staff could authenticate them without much trouble. People were talking like these baseballs could be worth as much as $1 million, and he wasn't about to see some little kid trampled in the crush to get the ball. Hallinan's staff began to use terms like "ticket integrity," when speaking about ways to keep fans in their assigned sections, and "crowd management," when considering how to block vendors from working the aisles when McGwire or Sosa were at bat. There was the first mention of "extraction teams," security personnel assigned to remove the ball and its new owner from the scene. Hallinan commissioned a statistical analysis of the home run histories and proclivities of both sluggers to determine the eventuality of balls being hit in certain areas. He did this knowing McGwire tended to hit his home runs pretty much in the same place each time out, and Sosa tended to spray them all over the field, but he wanted to be as thorough in his approach as possible. He consulted some of the top stadium operation people in the National and American Leagues, wanting their thoughts on what security programs had worked successfully in their ballparks.

In the end, Hallinan went with his gut and with what he already had. He pooled his in place Resident Security Agents, active duty police officers employed by Major League Baseball in every major league city, and assigned them to McGwire and Sosa details. On a full schedule, there were games in only fifteen ballparks on any given day, which meant that half his RSA force was available to travel to Cubs and Cardinals games and offer assistance. Hallinan's plan was to outfit these officers with white Major League Baseball jackets and caps and deploy them in strategic outfield locations. From these posts, they would be able to assist stadium ushers and team security personnel and the local police. They could circulate among the fans and get them thinking about safety issues and what might happen if a ball should come their way. They would also be able to implement Hallinan's crowd management and ticket integrity strategies, which were sometimes referred to as McGwire or Sosa "shifts." The word called to mind the defensive realignments managers put in place against can't-help-but-pull hitters like Willie McCovey and Dave Kingman, but it was more of a shutdown than a shift. No fan could go into or out of an outfield section without a corresponding ticket stub; no vendors could work in outfield sections during the half innings when McGwire or Sosa were due to bat; and no movement would be allowed in the aisles when they were at the plate.

"The fans who bought those seats had a right to be there," Hallinan said, "but they also had a right to be there safely."

For the tasks of marking and tracking the baseballs, Hallinan turned to Ruben Puente, a meticulous man who once worked the crime lab for the Arlington Police Department and was now a member of Hallinan's full-time staff. Puente quickly devised a way to mark all the balls to be pitched to McGwire sequentially, with a visible stamped number in footnote position atop the "s" of the Rawlings logo. In addition, he would mark the balls around the lacing with a distinct, invisible stamp, able to be seen under black or infrared light. His plan, once the leading home run hitter reached 59 home runs, was to put the first marked ball into play, and then the second, and the third, and so forth. If a ball left the field, the next in line took its place. If a ball was scuffed, or no longer suitable for game use, it was set aside for its succeeding number. Each ball would be tracked by one of Puente's associates, Linda Pantell, whose principal job was to bring the marked baseballs to each Cardinals game and record the fate of each ball in the series. If McGwire fouled one into the left field stands, Pantell would write it down. If he flied out to left, she'd write that down too.

To begin, Puente special ordered eight dozen baseballs direct from Rawlings on August 29, which were shipped directly to his office in Arlington from the company's Springfield, Missouri warehouse. The balls, according to codes burned into the underside of the cowhide covers at the Rawlings plant in Turrialba, Costa Rica, were manufactured in late June. Puente personally marked each ball in the sequence, and hand carried them to his suite at the Adam's Mark Hotel in downtown St. Louis, across the street from Busch Stadium. There, on Thursday, September 3, an off day, they were rubbed with Lena Blackburne's Rubbing Mud by Cardinals equipment manager Buddy Bates and his assistant Kurt Schlogl, while Puente and Pantell looked on. (Bates and Schlogl brought over a small tin of the mud from the Cardinals' equipment room, knowing the stuff probably wasn't available on the Adam's Mark room service menu.)

As each ball was rubbed, and as Bates and Schlogl dried their hands on hotel towels, Pantell numbered the slots in the sectioned Rawlings shipping box. She had the idea to place each ball in its matching slot, so that she and her colleagues could quickly determine their place in the sequence, and once the balls were rubbed and replaced, she fit the entire box into a small, wheeled suitcase, the kind a stewardess might carry on an overnight assignment.

By Friday, September 4, the first game of a weekend series against the Cincinnati Reds, the balls were ready—and just in time. McGwire had gone on a tear in Florida, hitting two home runs against the Marlins on September 1 and another two on September 2, bringing his season total to 59 and leaving Puente to wonder how it was he was nearly caught short. Sosa wouldn't hit his 59th until September 11 in Chicago, so for the moment the authentication effort was focused exclusively on McGwire. Later, when Sosa hit his 60th and 61st with unmarked balls, reporters and critics charged Major League Baseball with a subtle form of racism for focusing on McGwire's efforts over Sosa's.

Here again, Puente wondered at being caught short. It wasn't racism at all. It wasn't anything but not realizing how big this home run race had become, how much it meant, and to how many people. No one in his office had intended to keep marking the balls for the rest of the season. They thought they'd get to 62 and that would be it. That was the milestone. Maybe they'd reconnoiter and jump-start the effort at the end of the season, but it was never the plan to carry it out the entire way. People didn't realize the expense that went into an operation such as this. There was the cost of the balls, but that was minimal. There was the full-time attention of four members of Hallinan's staff: Puente, Pantell, Ed Petersen, and Al Williams. There were travel and hotel expenses for all five and for as many as 12 RSAs. With nearly another month to run in the season, the total costs for marking and security could reach into the six figures.

Ultimately, though, Hallinan decided to continue the effort and to extend it to the remaining Cubs games as well, dispatching two full security details to travel with McGwire and Sosa the rest of the way. Pantell and Williams continued with the Cardinals, and Puente headed the Cubs effort, and at one point there were two groups of eight RSAs on the home run detail. There were two sets of balls, too. Puente left behind enough of the original batch of marked balls to see Pantell and McGwire through, and he set off with Sosa and the Cubs and a new batch of balls. Like the McGwire lot, these were also marked sequentially, beginning with number one, but the invisible markings were unique. Puente didn't load up on these balls, however, because he was able to tag new balls from his hotel room on the road; he could even tag them during the game, if it came to that. He never knew how long the balls would last. They could go through a dozen balls in a single at bat, or they could last two games. As it happened, Sosa went through more balls than McGwire, on a relative basis.

"He kept fouling them off," Puente explained of Sosa. "McGwire was very frugal with his."

The St. Louis-based Rawlings Sporting Goods Company has been making baseballs the same way since 1977, when it was awarded the exclusive manufacturing contract for Major League Baseball. In fact, the baseballs have been essentially the same since 1931, when the Reach Sporting Goods Company, which was later bought by Spalding, developed the cushioned cork center to help the ball hold its shape. Prior to 1931, baseballs were known to flatten on one side if they were hit too hard; reports of routine fly balls wobbling through the air like misshapen eggs were not uncommon, but it took the notion of encasing two rubber shells around a small sphere of composition cork to end what is now known as the dead-ball era.

In the late 1800s, professional baseballs were not manufactured according to standard guidelines, which meant you could stuff pretty much anything you wanted between two pieces of leather, and if it somehow came out looking like a baseball it could find its way into a professional game. Typically, the home teams were responsible for supplying the balls, and a home team manager might run out a dead baseball when his team was in the field and a more lively baseball when his team was at the plate. Such were the nuances of the game (and the advantages of home field). Manufacturers advertised "the deadest balls made," in hopes of winning the business of defensive-minded teams. According to the first Official Baseball Guide, published in 1878, game-used balls became the property of the winning team, and budget-conscious equipment managers hoarded those early baseballs like rare tobacco cards; there was even a rule requiring umpires to suspend play for at least five minutes to look for a lost ball before putting a new one into play.

With no real guidelines in place and with dozens of suppliers lobbying for the business of big league clubs, the weight and circumference of balls varied widely—often from one inning to the next. By 1872, however, the ball reached today's standards: between 5 and $5\frac{1}{4}$ ounces in weight and 9 and $9\frac{1}{4}$ inches in circumference. Within those narrow constraints, 125 years later, there still exists a margin for error, and Rawlings baseballs are subject to a series of tests to ensure compliance with contemporary Major League Baseball regulations. Almost every ball is weighed, most are measured, and many are sampled—at various points throughout the assembly process. Out of every lot, several dozen balls are sent to Rawlings' quality control center in Ava, Missouri, where they are tested for C.O.R., or coefficient of restitution. The tested balls are like lab rats injected with toxins: There's no real hope for them after they're put through their paces. The balls are fired from an air cannon at a rate of 85 feet per second, or about 45 miles per hour, and shot against a wall made of northern white ash, the wood used in almost every major league baseball bat. If the ball rebounds at slightly more than half its initial velocity (.51 to .58 percent), it is deemed official. Clearly, the tested balls are no longer suitable for game use after such as this (unless it is a game to be played by lab rats), but the matching lot is shipped from holding bays in the company's Springfield, Missouri, warehouse to major league clubhouses around the country.

Rawlings supplies approximately 90,000 dozen baseballs each year to to major league baseball clubs. That's a lot of baseballs—over one million, give or take a couple dozen. Neither Rawlings, nor major league baseball officials, will reveal the wholesale price of a single ball, but it is understood to be about $5. (Internally, a team like the St. Louis Cardinals charges its players $5 for balls used for promotional giveaways or charitable donations.) The same ball is sold to the general public at sporting goods, hardware, drug, and department stores at prices ranging from $8 to $12.

Usually, a baseball will find its way into a game within two to three months of final assembly at the Rawlings plant in the small farming village of Turrialba, Costa Rica, an area known more for its sugarcane and macadamia nuts than for its contribution to the national pastime. Here, by the local soccer stadium (the official mailing address of the factory is "Behind the Rafael Camacho Stadium"), some five hundred workers put the finishing touches on as many as 1,000 dozen baseballs each day, all year long. It is a curious assembly line, drawing on materials from throughout the United States.

The ball's chief visible element, the grade one cowhide leather that holds the ball together, is purchased through the A. Mindel & Sons hide brokerage in Toledo, Ohio, which gets its goods from cattle farms and slaughterhouses throughout the midwest. The hides are then shipped on flatbed trucks—on palettes stacked fifty high—to the Rawlings-owned Tennessee Tanning

Company, in Tullahoma, Tennessee, where they are cured, soaked, stretched, tanned, and cut into the figure eight-shaped swatches that will become the balls' stitched together covers. Hides used during the 1998 baseball season were purchased at market prices ranging from $40 to $64. The "harvest" on each hide, after stretching, yields approximately twenty-two square feet of usable leather, which in turn yields a matched set of covers for about seven dozen baseballs. That's roughly thirteen thousand hides for the season, allowing for trim waste and deficiencies in the grain.

The leather, a by-product of the dairy and meat packing industries, comes mostly from holstein and guernsey cows, the hides of which tend to be thin and offer a fairly large surface area for cutting. (Until 1974, the balls were held together by horsehide, when a supply problem caused a run-up in prices and a hardly acknowledged shift to routine.) The cowhides arrive in Tullahoma in a green-salted condition, after having been cured in a brine solution to kill bacteria. At the tannery, the hides are soaked and rehydrated in a fresh water-based detergent, and unhaired with a chemical process to break down the hair protein keratin. The leather is then tanned with an aluminum sulfate tannage to give it the natural white color of a from-the-box baseball, and even then, the folks at the tannery will have to add some pigment to get the color just right.

Mike Cunningham, plant manager of Rawlings' Tennessee tannery, tells how in the Book of Matthew, in the New Testament, the tanner was made to live on the outskirts of the city, because the work was so dirty. No one wanted this guy around. It is still very much an ugly business, Cunningham says, and it's hard to get clean, but it's the kind of ugly business that gets in your blood. It's like railroading, he says. Most people grow up around it, they don't mind it too much.

Ironically, or perhaps just coincidentally, Heath Wiseman, the young veterinary student who caught Mark McGwire's 68th home run ball, was raised on a 1,500-acre cattle farm in Bryant, South Dakota. As a kid, he never thought of the cattle on his farm in terms of the baseballs he played with, or even the glove he wore, until it was about wore out. This strikes Wiseman now as somewhat surprising, seeing how baseball played as big a part in his growing up as cattle. For a time, he roamed center field for an amateur baseball team not far from his hometown. He supposes he always knew, on some level, that the gloves and balls of the game he loved flowed at least in some secondary way from the farm he worked with his father, but he never thought about it much.

To Wiseman, the couple hundred head of cattle on his father's farm represented steaks and hamburgers and roasts, and at a certain point he knew to consider how the internal organs might be ground into hot dogs and liver and sausage casings. The cows would go to slaughter—at anywhere from $700 to $1,000 for a fattened-out steer— and the hides would be ripped off by these huge machines, but it wasn't until September 26, 1998, seventh inning, second to last game of the season, one on, two outs, when McGwire sent his 68th and, for the time being, ultimate home run of the season into Wiseman's black Rawlings glove that he made the connection. It was, he doesn't mind saying, a pretty nice grab.

At the Costa Rica plant, a thin coating of rubber cement is applied to the cushioned cork center, which is placed on a machine and wrapped with a tight winding of four-ply gray wool. The first wrap is topped by a three-ply tan wool, a three-ply gray wool, and finally a thin poly-cotton thread that essentially gives the ball its shape. That's four windings in all, and according to Rawlings promotion representative Aaron Boutwell, you could probably put the leather cover on the ball after the first three, but you wouldn't get a perfect round sphere the way you do with the cotton layer. After a while, it would look like one of those misshapen eggs from the game's early days.

The four wool and cotton windings are all made with different colors, to allow for quick visual inspection. Even the cushioned cork center is put together with two different-colored rubber sections, one red and one black, to allow for the same kind of spot-check, and balls are sliced at statistically representative intervals to make sure they are being made properly. One of the things that gets to a guy like Boutwell, whose job it sometimes is to explain to school groups how baseballs are made, is the way people talk about the ball being "juiced," or wound too tight. When you think about it, which he is paid to do, you realize such claims don't make sense. Sure, if the ball is wound too tight, it's likely to travel a greater distance with the same impact, but what people don't realize is a too-tight winding means a corresponding difference in the amount of wool, which would change the weight and circumference of the ball. If you change one of the variables, it invariably changes another.

Next, the precisely-wound ball is trimmed of excess tailings and rubbed with another thin coating of rubber cement before two cowhide covers are puzzled together to complete the sphere. The covers are then stitched, by hand, with waxed red thread. It takes 108 stitches, 2 needles, 88 inches of waxed red thread, and about five minutes for one person to complete the job.

After the cover is sewn, the ball is placed in a rolling machine for about fifteen seconds to flatten the seams and ensure a uniform surface. For a time, Rawlings worked with several machines designed to eliminate the hand-stitching step of the process but could never replicate the human element needed to keep the stitches taut and level. To some, the inconsistencies in the hand-sewing process provide the essential difference between professional models and high school and college balls. In amateur ball, where aluminum bats offer a measurable advantage to the hitter, it's thought that the pitchers are better able to compete with raised, uneven seams. A raised-seam ball breaks bigger—and, therefore, better—which is why you'll sometimes see a great college pitcher with a killer curveball never make it to the big leagues. He'll do just fine with the seams to his advantage, but as soon as they're rolled and flattened, he loses his edge and his pitches wind up on the other side of the fence.

The only difference between the major league balls and the National and American League balls are cosmetic: The colors of the waxed thread and the ink used in stamping. National League balls are stamped in black ink; American League balls, in blue. For All-Star games, two different colored threads are used, representing the colors of the host team, and stitched in an alternating pattern. World Series balls, in even years, are red; in odd years, blue.

In all, the hard costs of cork, rubber, wool, polycotton thread, waxed thread, and leather run less than two dollars per ball. Labor brings up the cost by another dollar or so, and the company gets a lot of manpower for that extra buck: At least two dozen sets of hands touch the ball and its component parts in production. The hides alone are handled by about a dozen people before they are cut and shipped to Costa Rica. In Turrialba, there are four different loadings of yarn, onto four different machines, by four different people. There's one person to apply the glue to the pill, and another to apply the glue to the cover. There's someone to do the stitching, someone to take the ball onto the floor to be stamped, and someone to take it to the machine to be rolled. Then there are the folks who pack the ball and prepare it for shipping.

The ball is complete when it leaves the Turrialba plant for Rawlings' warehouse in Springfield, but it's not ready for game use until it's rubbed with a pinch of mud, and not just any mud will do. Lena Blackburne's Baseball Rubbing Mud, the mysterious compound dredged from the shores of New Jersey's Pennsauken Creek, a tributary to the Delaware River, has been the "unofficial" rubbing mud of Major League Baseball for more than a half century, since journeyman infielder-turned-manager Blackburne stumbled across the mud on a fishing trip. The mud is the stuff of baseball legend. The precise location of the mud bank is a closely held secret. The mud is collected once a year, late at night, by the extended members of a single family working by flashlight, after which it's carted off in 55-gallon drums, processed, and dispatched to big league clubhouses in nondescript, one pound coffee cans donated by neighbors.

The art and practice of mud rubbing dates to the 1920s, after Cleveland shortstop Ray Chapman was killed by a wild pitch and umpires were directed to put fresh balls into play at regular intervals during the game. The problem with this rule, however, was that pitchers complained about the slick grip on the always-new baseballs. Then, as now, it takes a couple kicks in the dirt for the leather on a fresh ball to lose its slickness after being tanned. League officials decided that if the balls were rubbed with mud before each game it would dull the sheen from the leather and protect the players from any errant throws, especially in the wet weather that did in poor Chapman. At first, this was done with an on-the-fly solution of infield dirt and tobacco juice. It eventually fell to the umpires to rub down ten to twelve dozen balls before each game—a tedious task that soon became a kind of rite of passage for the ball boys and clubhouse assistants who've taken on the umpire's job in exchange for tips.

The main trick is to get the slickness off the ball without taking the whiteness with it. The side trick is to work quickly because it's grunt work. Kurt Schlogl, the assistant equipment manager for the St. Louis Cardinals who helped rub the record-territory baseballs marked by league officials and pitched to Mark McGwire and Sammy Sosa down the stretch, tells how it's not as easy as it sounds, this rubbing business. Either the balls are too light or too dark, or the surface comes out splotchy or uneven. Nowadays, the umps are as concerned with how a ball looks on television as how it feels in their hands.

Blackburne's mud is said to contain just the right amounts of silt and sand and is relatively free of gravel. Several companies have analyzed the reddish brown compound and developed their own versions for commercial use, but the umpires stand behind the Blackburne stuff. That is, they stand behind it when and where they can get their hands in a coffee can full. In the low minors, when and where they cannot, umpires must sometimes make do, and National League umpire Richard Rieker reports that when he was in the bushes he would go out to the parking lot before each game and rub up game balls with the dirt alongside his car. This was especially convenient for some umpires in that they could sit in their cars and listen to the radio as they did the work, if they were so inclined. Rieker, who was behind the plate when McGwire hit his 70th home run of the 1998 season, can't tell you how many times he cut up his hands before a minor league game. It's hard to believe all the broken glass they've got in some of those parking lots.

Finally, the baseball is ready to be put into play. And yet for all of the labor and hard material costs, for all the testing and inspecting, for all the planning and rubbing, each individual ball has a surprisingly short life span: six pitches. Sometimes more, sometimes less, but that's basically it. Three to four weeks to turn a hide into a cut cover, one to two months to fully assemble a ball from its component parts, all those busy hands being paid by the piece, and the ball's job is done after just a couple minutes.

The official rules of baseball, article 3.01 (d), require only "one dozen regulation reserve balls to be immediately available for use if required," although standard practice calls for ten times that amount. Of course, the law of averages being what they are, and baseball being the game of statistical probability that it is, it's entirely possible that one dozen reserve balls might someday be enough, in some game, somewhere, if the ball never leaves the field of play. It's possible, but not likely. There is one modern-era game on the books—an August 4, 1908 contest between the St. Louis Cardinals and the Brooklyn Superbas—in which a full nine innings were played with only one game ball, but for the most part, it's up and out and on to the next one.

One million baseballs per season.

Ten dozen balls per game.

Seven dozen balls per hide—or, a little more than one cow per game.

Six pitches per ball.

Rawlings' Boutwell helps to put the effort into perspective. The folks at Rawlings, he says, they're fans just like anyone else. They go to the games and people ask them who they're rooting for, and they say they're rooting for the ball. For them, it's a no-lose situation. The ball always has a good game. It's the cow who's not having one of her better days.

The caretaking of the marked McGwire and Sosa balls was a constant worry to a detail-oriented guy like Ruben Puente. Don't misunderstand him, he was always thinking clearly, but the mistakes he usually caught on second check were somehow slipping by to a third. One near gaffe stood out. Sosa's 65th was a big fly to center that landed in the "batter's eye" in Milwaukee County Stadium—the closed-off section of seats that were kept empty to leave a solid backdrop for the hitters. It bounced back onto the field and was retrieved by Brewers center fielder Marquis Grissom, who returned it to the umpire. The ball made its way to Puente in the middle of such postgame confusion that he sent a message to Sosa informing him that the ball was safe and that he would give it to him the next day. The Cubs were headed to Houston that night, and Puente was due to make the trip as well, so he figured he would save Sosa the trouble of traveling with the ball.

The next night was equally chaotic, and this time

Sosa sent a message to Puente to hold onto the ball for another day. When Puente left the Astrodome, however, something caught his attention. There was a small crowd gathered around the players' entrance, jockeying for autographs, and Puente noticed a boy at the back of the scrum, wanting to be let in. It was an ordinary, orderly pack of fans, and the smaller kids were always being pushed to the back, but something struck Puente about this one little boy. He was about eight years old, and he seemed to Puente about the happiest kid on the planet. He didn't care that he was being muscled out of position for an autograph. He was just glad to be out at the ballpark.

Puente couldn't say what possessed him, but he remembered he had an extra ball in his briefcase. It wasn't a game ball, but it was an official ball, and he pulled his car over to where the crowd had formed and motioned for the kid. He reached into his briefcase for the ball and held it out to him. "Here, son," he said to the kid. "I want you to have this. It's from Major League Baseball."

Just then, Puente thought to give the ball a final once-over before handing it to the boy. He looked down, and lost a breath. It was Sosa's baseball! He'd reached inside his briefcase and picked out the wrong ball, so he kicked himself over what nearly happened and reached back in for the unmarked ball. And do you know what? It might as well have been the Sosa ball, from the way the kid started smiling and hollering and going ballistic. Puente made sure to tell him it was just an ordinary baseball, but the kid didn't care. It was a brand-new official baseball, and it was the greatest thing in the world.

For Puente, it turned out to be one of those priceless, what-the-game-is-all-about kind of moments, and yet when he leaned back into his car he was shaken. He was with three RSAs, and one of them noticed he was a little pale. He explained to his colleagues how he'd almost given away Sosa's ball by mistake, and the three men had a good laugh.

"Ruben," one of them said, "you're probably the only guy in the world, if you had given it to him, you could just go back to your hotel room and make another. No one would ever know."

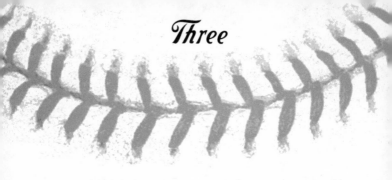

Three

Let's Make
a Deal

*Or, One Person's Memorabilia Is
Another Person's Sporting Good*

In some respects, the buying and selling of the record home run balls of 1998 offered a short course in the market timing of wasting assets. At the moment each was hit, and retrieved, it was arguably the most valuable ball to ever leave the field of play, but with each subsequent home run that value would undoubtedly shrink. By September, the game within the game had become the constant figuring on what these balls might be worth at season's end, and for what reasons.

On September 1, in Miami, when McGwire tied Hack Wilson's sixty-eight-year-old National League record with his 56th of the season, a 450-foot shot to center in the seventh inning off Marlins pitcher Livan Hernandez, the market was established. The ball was caught by eleven-year-old Jason Duncan of Fort Lauderdale, who traded it back to McGwire after the game, through a Cardinals' representative, for two signed bats, two signed balls, a signed jersey, and six tickets to the next day's game. Two innings later, seventeen-year-old Michael Pitt of Fort Meyers caught McGwire's 57th, and he cut himself the same deal. Both fans reportedly turned down $5,000 cash offers from the same unidentified collector.

The game was afoot.

Sosa, for his part, wasn't playing. A copy editor for *The Chicago Tribune* caught Sosa's 56th, hit the next day in Chicago off Cincinnati's Jason Bere, but when she tried to give it to the Cubs' right fielder after the game, he simply signed it and handed it back. Sosa did the same thing two days later, in Pittsburgh, when an unidentified young fan tried to present him with the ball he'd hit for his 57th home run, which had set a single-season Cubs' record, breaking Wilson's mark. Imagine that! observers marveled. An athlete who believed the artifacts of his accomplishments belonged with the fans who retrieved them. I am a ballplayer, Sosa seemed to say. Let someone else worry where these should go.

When the Cardinals returned to St. Louis later that week, the fans in the outfield seats were ready for the grand prizes—and a great many of them would have traded those prizes for whatever was hiding behind door number three. It had become the trend to give the balls back to the men who hit them and soak in whatever good will and signed merchandise came as a result.

On September 5, McGwire sent a 2–0 fastball from Cincinnati's Dennis Reyes into the left field seats just inside the foul pole, where it was retrieved by a St. Louis Rams employee, twenty-two-year-old Deni Allen of Maryland Heights, Missouri. McGwire now stood in the good company of Ruth and Maris as the only ballplayers to hit 60 home runs in a single season, and Allen held out for a little something more in honor of the occasion: a signed ball, two signed bats, two season tickets, and the chance to suit up in a Cardinals uniform and take batting practice with McGwire and his teammates.

Sports reporters around the country, running out of things to talk about, made sure to mention that the ball was marked by Major League Baseball with the number three, just to the right of the cursive "s" on the Rawlings' stamp, representing the third marked and coded ball thrown to McGwire down the stretch, as well as the uniform number of Babe Ruth, the first man to reach the 60 home run mark. Major League Baseball's Kevin Hallinan noticed the empty #3 slot in the Rawlings box in Linda Pantell's suitcase and smiled to himself, thinking, *Hey Babe, I know you're here somewhere.*

Writers and commentators also found time to praise Allen and McGwire as exemplars of what the sport should be about—giving back, unselfish play, preserving the game for future generations—while sideline observers wondered what it was about baseball that placed such high-minded burdens on its fans and participants. Allen, despite holding out for the toughest barter terms to date, followed the unfolding script and told reporters the ball would have burned a hole in his heart if he had hung on to it. (Nice line.) Collectors offering tens of thousands of dollars for the 60th home run ball were roundly vilified for representing the base instincts of our culture. All was right with the baseball world.

The conversation around watercoolers that Monday morning was for the most part ennobling, uplifting. How refreshing, it was widely thought, to see everyone's head screwed on just right, to see these valuable artifacts returned to the National Baseball Hall of Fame and Museum in Cooperstown, New York, where they belonged. On the Mike and the Mad Dog afternoon call-in show on WFAN-AM in New York callers were openly supportive of Deni Allen and his decision to give back the ball. Most said they would have done the same thing. On KFNS-AM, the leading sports radio station in St. Louis, hosts and callers took turns praising Allen, and the entire Cardinals organization, for showing the good sense in doing whatever it took to keep the ball on public display. It wouldn't hurt anybody, this kid's suiting up and taking b.p. He deserved whatever he could get. He was doing a good thing.

Jeff Idelson, executive director of the Hall, trailed McGwire and Sosa during the month of September, but unlike the collectors and the Cardinals he was in no position to bargain. He was just in position. The Hall of Fame does not pay for its items on display, although savvy benefactors have been known to receive lifetime passes to the museum, which might come in handy if they happened to live anywhere near Cooperstown. Mindful of how little he had to offer in return, Idelson considered himself fortunate that McGwire and Sosa had such a keen sense of baseball history, because at least he could trade on that. Both sluggers were quick to turn over the balls in their possession, along with related game-used items. All Idelson had to do, really, was stay out of the way.

McGwire's 61st and record-tying home run—a first-inning blast off Cubs starter Mike Morgan on Monday, September 7—was an upper deck job snared by a fan named Mike Davidson, who also traded the ball back to McGwire for signed items. The moment was memorable for a number of reasons beyond the feat itself: It pitted the two challengers to the home run crown on the same field, with Sosa stuck for the time being on his 58th home run. (When Sosa singled later in the game, the two shared a laugh and a hug at McGwire's post at first base, and then the Cub reportedly turned to the Cardinal and said, "Now you have to wait for me.") It provided news editors with a built-in dramatic hook, with the Roger Maris family seated behind the Cardinals dugout. And, in the kind of freakish coincidence that might some day rival the freakish coincidences surrounding, oh, the Kennedy and Lincoln assassinations—or not—Mark McGwire's father, John, was in attendance celebrating his 61st birthday.

After the game, much was made about what a rare and gentlemanly thing it was for two such fierce competitors to congratulate each other so graciously, how generous it was of McGwire to share the spotlight with the Maris family, and how difficult it will be for him to shop for his father in subsequent years.

By now, the Cardinals and Major League Baseball had this give-back program nailed to routine. Uniformed St. Louis police officers were assigned to roam the outfield stands throughout the game, with instructions to extract any fan lucky enough to grab a McGwire home run from his or her seat as quickly and unobtrusively as possible. Baseball's Resident Security Agents, the Hall of Fame, and venturesome collectors were also jockeying for position. More than once, an aggressive speculator gave chase as the ball-catching fan was whisked to an elevator in a motorized cart, only to have the elevator doors close on his proposals for an instant sale. Safe from interruption in a private room, a team representative would ask if the fan would like to return the ball to McGwire, in exchange for some signed items. A meeting would be arranged. McGwire would pose for pictures, the ball would be authenticated by Major League Baseball's Ruben Puente or Linda Pantell, the fan would be hurried to the radio booth for an interview with Jack Buck and Mike Shannon, and all concerned would go home richer for the experience.

Or, at least, that was the idea.

The very next day, McGwire stroked his 62nd and shortest home run of the season, a 341-foot screamer down the left field line off Chicago starter Steve Trachsel that barely cleared the wall. The ball landed in an open area beneath the stands and bounded around for a bit until it was retrieved by Tim Forneris, a member of the Busch Stadium grounds crew, while McGwire missed first base and had to double back before completing his home run trot for the ages. Play was stopped for eleven minutes, during which McGwire climbed into the stands to embrace the Maris family, and took the microphone to address the crowd of 49,987. He also found time to jump up and down and hug a few people he probably didn't know.

Here, at last, the Cardinals' informal policy on employees being allowed to keep a record ball with the club's blessing would be tested, but Forneris proved to be a team player. (His mother also worked for the Cardinals, so it's likely he had no choice, or risk being sent to his room.) There was never any question, Forneris said, but that ball belonged to McGwire. It belonged in the Hall of Fame. "Mr. McGwire," Forneris said in returning the ball in a postgame ceremony, "I found something that belongs to you." Forneris was later given a Cardinal-red minivan by a local Chrysler dealer, in a photo opportunity disguised as a show of gratitude, and the record ball was on its way to Cooperstown the following morning.

No one was happier with the young groundskeeper's generosity than the Hall of Fame's Idelson, who had visited with McGwire in the clubhouse before the game and brought with him the bat Roger Maris had used to hit his 61st home run thirty-seven years earlier. According to Idelson, McGwire looked the bat up and down, rubbed the barrel over the Cardinal logo on his jersey chest, and said, "Roger, I hope you're with me tonight."

It was an eerie feeling for Idelson to sit through the game with Maris's bat in his hands. He was in the press box, for the most part, and a lot of people had no real idea what he was holding. He carried the bat in a special case, and it could have been a pool cue, or a musical instrument—that is, it could have been a pool cue or musical instrument if those were the sorts of things people normally toted around the Busch Stadium press box. He couldn't stop thinking about it, all game long. He felt like he was in two places at the same time, whenever McGwire came to bat. He was there, in the press box, pulling for McGwire, and he was down in the stands, behind first base, a part of the Maris family. He wouldn't want anyone to think he was crazy or anything, but it was like he was in a parallel universe, holding Maris's bat while McGwire broke the record. One hand on the past, one hand on the present. It was certainly an unusual perspective.

When Idelson went to see him in the clubhouse after the postgame ceremony, McGwire was so overcome with emotion he couldn't get out of his clothes fast enough.

He was wearing history, and everything had to go. His uniform, his belt, his batting glove, his spikes . . . he wanted Idelson to take it all back to the Hall, along with the ball from Forneris and the bat he had used to hit home runs 57 through 62. He also donated the jersey worn by his ten-year-old son Matt, who had flown in from California to serve as ball boy for these historic games.

Idelson couldn't ship the items to Cooperstown (it's against the Hall's policy), so the plan was for him to personally carry them back to the museum. He might as well have asked for McGwire's equipment bag, to cart everything in.

A police detail was called the following morning, to escort Idelson and Hall of Fame president Don Maher to the airport, and they were met in Albany by New York state troopers, who escorted them to Cooperstown. The items were placed on display the next day, as part of an exhibit entitled "The March on Maris" that had opened before Labor Day weekend, marking one of the fastest turnarounds in the museum's rich history. Here again, this was a first for Idelson. No one at the Hall could remember a time when the thirst to eyeball such historic artifacts had reached such fanatical proportions, nor a time when the museum's own curators felt such a public pull to rush items into display.

It was an amazing thing, to stand back in the room where the exhibit was mounted. To have the shirt off McGwire's back, the bat from his hands, less than forty-eight hours after the event, it was a real coup. Idelson would look on at the 62nd home run ball and think that this was maybe why he took the job in the fist place.

He didn't know it, but it would be the last ball he'd see for the next while.

John Grass had never been to a game like the 62nd home run game. It wasn't just the record—although, you know, that was memorable enough. It was everything else. He has to tell you, it was probably the most exciting day he'd ever spent at the ballpark, and at forty-six, a Cardinals fan his whole life, he'd spent a lot of them.

The tickets were a luxury Grass couldn't always afford on a school district groundskeeper's salary, and especially not if the Cardinals were putting a lousy team on the field. But now that McGwire was in town, Grass kept finding reasons to go to the park. Back in June, he knew McGwire would make a run on the home run record. He just knew. He's not saying he's psychic, and he's not saying he was any different from anyone else in St. Louis, but he had a feeling, and he went out and bought left field bleacher tickets to every home game for the month of September.

The 62nd home run game was one crazy, unbelievable thing after another. First of all, the whole place was just pumping with excitement after McGwire hit it out. It was definitely something to see. The way they stopped the game, the way he climbed into the stands, the whole thing. But then a bunch of other stuff started happening. Ray Lankford caught a ball to end an inning and tossed it up into the stands. Grass was standing on his seat, beer in hand, and somehow managed to catch the ball. The moment he caught it, a collector came up to him and offered $200 for it. Grass figured, hey $200 is $200, and he sold it, like a dummy, because after that he spent the rest of the game trying to buy it back. A couple innings later, he wound up buying a similar ball from a young fan for $80—same circumstances, last out of the inning, outfielder being a good guy—and managed to convince the collector to make a trade. In the end, he wound up with the ball he originally caught, and a little extra money besides.

One week later, Grass went back to the stadium for a double-header against the Pirates. McGwire wasn't playing in the first game, but Grass had a feeling something big was gonna happen. It was easy to say this later, but he could back it up. J. D. Drew came to bat, and Grass turned to his buddies and said, "This guy's gonna hit a home run." Drew, the multi-million-dollar bonus baby who held out for big bucks when the Phillies claimed him in the amateur draft, had joined the Cardinals just a few weeks earlier and St. Louis fans were anxious for him to bust out and have a big game. And what did this guy do? He hit a home run, just like Grass predicted. But that was nothing. When Drew came up again, Grass turned and said the same thing. Mind you, he wasn't saying this every time a guy came to the plate, just Drew, and the rookie hit another one out. Two times in a row, calling the kid's shots like that, that was a whole lot more than nothing.

Finally, ninth inning, LaRussa sent McGwire out to pinch-hit for second baseman Delino Deshields and Grass's good buddy Larry Thomas turned to him and said, "Okay, know-it-all, what's he gonna do?"

Grass looked over at his pal, completely serious, and said, "He's gonna hit a home run and it's comin' to us."

One ball, no strikes, McGwire smacked his 63rd home run so hard you could hear the pop out in the bleachers. Thomas looked up and said, "Here it comes."

Grass will always see the picture in his mind, looking up to find the ball in the night sky. It was drizzling, and the ball kinda hung in the lights. The rain looked like more than it really was, coming down around those light poles. It was a towering shot, real high, and Grass started to think it was like that part in *The Natural*, when the ball just blows and blows and keeps going. It took forever to find its way back down—ten minutes, if he had to guess—but Grass never moved his eyes off that ball. He held his ground, watching the ball, standing on his bleacher seat, and at the last minute he kicked up on his toes and reached out with his glove and made the grab. The glove sucked the ball tight into the pocket, swallowed it right up, almost without a sound, and Grass screamed, "I've got it!" He felt like he was ten years old, and it was Christmas, and he was opening presents.

Next thing he knew, he was punched twice on the side of the head, and next thing after that, he was up in the press box, him and Larry, thinking through their next move. It was between games of the doubleheader. The Cardinals, they'd already worked their number on him, telling Grass how McGwire would really like the ball, how the other fans had been trading the balls for signed items. Grass knew what those other guys had gotten, it was a whole lot more than signed items, so he thought along those lines. Plus, he knew that half of whatever he got for the ball would go to his friend Larry. It wasn't even a handshake deal with them. They were best friends, and they shared everything. If they went gambling, they split the pot down the middle. This ball was no different.

Grass decided to make a list, to keep everything straight in his mind. He borrowed a piece of paper and a pen from a *St. Louis Post-Dispatch* writer, and he started writing:

2 Stan the Man jerseys, signed

3 bats each, signed

3 caps each, signed

3 jerseys each (XL), signed

3 gloves each, signed

3 balls each, signed

2 Cardinals jackets (XL), signed

3 pictures each, signed

4 season tickets, section 591, bleachers

4 round-trip tickets to Jupiter, Florida for spring training, and one week's hotel accommodations

John & John throw out first ball on September 26

1 bat and ball, signed, for every member of family

Truth was, Grass wasn't married to any of it. He wasn't asking for money, and the Florida trip was just something he threw in. They didn't want to go to Disney World or lie on the beach. They wanted to see the Cardinals play. And as far as throwing out the first pitch, well, that was as much for Grass's son John as it was for him. He's twenty-one, John, and he could have been a pretty decent pitcher, Grass was convinced. The kid could throw in the upper 80s, and it's been a disappointment to Grass that he never developed. It's who you know, even in baseball. It's politics. They're looking for kids who can throw in the 90s, but there are a lot of top pitchers don't throw in the 90s, so you tell Grass it's not politics.

Cardinal vice president William O. DeWitt, III took one look at Grass's list and couldn't tell if this guy was serious. It was the sheer *volume* of what he was requesting, more than it was any one thing. The team might have been able to live with him or his kid throwing out the first ball, if that was what it took. They'd already let Deni Allen take batting practice, so that precedent had been set. It's possible they could have even lived with the four season tickets—it wasn't like the guy wanted dugout box seats, or field box; he wanted bleacher seats. The spring training trip was a problem however, because the club didn't want to be in the business of actually paying out money for these home run balls. If it was a barter item, then maybe they could work something out.

Grass said later he never expected to get every item, but he was hoping at least for a chance to negotiate. It wasn't a list of demands, like it was reported in the press. He wasn't holding the ball hostage. The list was just a place to start. If it seemed like a good idea, he put it down.

Still, the Cardinals took Grass back to meet McGwire after the second game of the doubleheader. At that point, McGwire was meeting all the ball holders, and the expectation was they would acquiesce. McGwire was real nice about it, Grass recalled. He said, "You want a couple balls, a couple bats?"

Grass said, "Well, no, actually, it's a little more than that." He showed him the list. He's a good-size man, John Grass, built low to the ground, like a football player, with the chiseled good looks and matinee-grey hair of some rugged guy in a cigarette advertisement, but next to an athlete like McGwire he felt relatively small. The first baseman reached for the piece of paper Grass handed to him, and his arms looked like a couple logs you'd throw on a fire.

McGwire looked the list over and handed it back. He didn't smile. He was still nice about it, but maybe a little more formal. It was like a switch was flipped, and he knew he wasn't gonna get the ball. Grass explained how he came from a big family, how he knew McGwire himself was a big family man, how he was trying to take care of his own. You'd think he'd understand a thing like that. The new home run king said he was not in a position to negotiate. He told Grass to talk to general manager Walt Jocketty, or someone from the front office, and the two men shook hands and parted.

Over the next few hours, the list became one of the more talked-about sidebars to McGwire's lead, notable for the way it broke from form and the absolute gumption it seemed to represent on its face. McGwire's late season home runs had each received significant play in the St. Louis press, but Grass's "holdout" was treated like a breaking story. Reporters figured Grass for the first villain in what had been a fairly saccharine tale of baseball tradition and making nice. The Cardinals promised to get back to Grass, but they seemed to have no intention of doing so. It wasn't a front burner matter to them, DeWitt said later. There'd be other balls, and the list was out of hand.

By the time the story hit the local news shows later that night, it was as if Grass's version of events had been passed through a children's game of Telephone before finding its way into print or on the air. The way it was reported, Grass had gone out to the ballpark with the list already written. He and his friends had chosen their seats strategically, to maximize their chances of catching the ball. None of these things was a crime, but they were reported as if Grass was a scheming beast. He *planned* to catch the ball, the story went. He and his buddies actually *spread out*, to cover more ground. He was taking advantage of McGwire's generosity. He was making the good people of St. Louis look seedy, second-rate. One radio station reported that Grass wanted to throw out the first ball at every remaining home game. Who the hell was he, a goddamn maintenance worker for a local school district, calling the shots? Didn't he realize that as soon as McGwire hit another one his ball would be worthless?

By morning, Grass was the most hated man in all of St. Louis. If not the most hated, then at least the most misunderstood, and if not the most misunderstood in St. Louis history then at least the most misunderstood since Lindbergh. People left threatening messages on his answering machine. Sports radio talk show hosts called him greedy. He was the devil, in Cardinal red. Grass tried to tune out all the talk, but it was impossible. The kids at the schools where he worked, they all knew about it. His own kids were hearing all kinds of things. Even the guys at the pizza place in his neighborhood had something to say about it.

The next night, at Busch, well-dressed teenagers handed out fliers with the message "Give the Ball Back to Mac" in big letters. The flier was printed up by The Motley Fool investment advising team, which runs a column in the *St. Louis Post-Dispatch*. "If you want millions of dollars," the fine print read, "save your money and learn how to invest it." Grass took it personally. He laughed it off, but it rankled. He hated the way people were talking about him. He hated for his family to have to listen to it. He hated that he hadn't heard back from the Cardinals. He hated that this wonderful, unlikely thing happened, that he actually caught the kind of home run ball that might be talked about for years, and he couldn't enjoy it.

He'd never meant to do the wrong thing, but at this point John Grass had no idea what the right thing might be. If it was true what people were saying, about how much this ball might be worth, he'd have to be crazy to trade it away for a few bats and balls. He'd been prepared to play it that way, but the more he thought about it the more he began to question it. One million dollars. That kind of money was so far off the radar screen of a guy who makes $30,000 a year, cutting and lining the playing fields of the city's schools, that it didn't make sense. He'd have given up the ball in a heartbeat, if the Cardinals had just dealt with him decently, if McGwire had said they could work something out, but now he was glad that didn't happen.

John Grass knew he would never get to throw out a ball at Busch Stadium, but he had in his possession one of the most notorious balls to ever leave its premises.

Mike Barnes couldn't tell you where he was when the notion first hit, but the twenty-eight-year-old agent with an unusual client mix of fine artists and extreme athletes had started to look on these home run balls as the kind of opportunity that only came around once or twice in a career. Problem was, it was an opportunity he couldn't quite get inside to see—until John Grass left the door open a crack.

Barnes drove to work Wednesday morning, September 16, as he listened to the talk on KFNS, and he couldn't understand why people were beating up on this poor groundskeeper. They were massacring this guy, for the simple crime of keeping something that was by all rights his. When you play the lottery, and your numbers come in, nobody in the least expects you to give the money back to the lottery commission or to donate it to charity. In this case, though, that was exactly what these people were saying John Grass should do. Barnes didn't get it. Baseball had been telling people, for eighty years, that if you bring your kid to the game he could catch a ball. People bring their gloves to the ballpark. And now, when these balls might suddenly be worth hundreds of thousands of dollars, the feeling was that they should be returned. There was even a not-so-subtle type of pressure being exerted, outside the stadium, outside the game itself, by the fans. Why is that? Barnes wondered.

In the last few weeks, like almost everyone else in St. Louis, Barnes had been fixed to every Cardinals game, to see what McGwire might do. He'd watch the games with his four-year-old son Alexander and imagine a role for himself in all the excitement. He started to realize that where these balls were hit, out in the bleachers, you were seeing a class of fans that for the most part couldn't afford to pass up what these balls might represent. He heard about the $1 million offer, for the record-setting ball. He didn't get why these people were so quick to give these balls back to McGwire. These weren't people sitting in luxury or corporate boxes. These were people for whom the balls might have meant a college education for one of their kids, or the chance at a bigger house in a nicer neighborhood. These were groundskeepers and students (and, as it turned out, people who worked in the tire industry). Barnes had as much of a sense of baseball history as the next guy, but there was no logic to this kind of thinking, at least not on that kind of socioeconomic scale.

Barnes was inclined to look at things from a social standpoint. He would work a problem and try to fully understand it before attempting to solve it. It was an approach that informed his career and the way he lived his life. He joined organizations like the Enlightenment Forum and the Top One Percent Society (or, TOPS), because he felt an association with like-minded people might give him an advantage. He went to law school, but he never meant to be a lawyer. He liked the action too much to have to grind out contracts in a corporate setting, to have to work for someone else. He dreaded the thought of spending his life punching a clock. He wanted to be working the phones, out in the field, creating wealth and opportunities for himself and his clients, so he decided to become an agent. Sports, entertainment, commercials . . . there were all kinds of possibilities. Barnes had seen that show *Arliss*, on HBO; he'd read about people like David Falk and Michael Ovitz. He knew he could carve out a comfortable lifestyle for his young family if he could make a thorough analysis of the field, and catch a few breaks. If things really went his way, he could operate from his base in St. Louis, a place not known for its wealth of big time sports and entertainment agencies.

He actually market researched himself into a niche, first in the art community and then in sports. He started representing fine artists, running interference for them with gallery owners and dealers, and his client list quickly grew to about fifty painters and sculptors, including the noted American impressionist Max Scharf. Barnes's impulse to generate money didn't always fit with the artists' impulses to make a statement. Once, a political expressionist told Barnes he would never allow his work to be sold to a corporation, and he wanted a sociological profile of any buyer to ensure that their sensibilities and beliefs were compatible with his own. It was the most ridiculous thing Barnes had ever heard. The guy needed to sell his work to live, and here he was putting all these conditions on any sale.

In sports, the issues were somewhat more clear: Make as much money as you can for your clients, as quickly as you can, and help them to keep their image consistent with their sport and with their product. The problem here, though, was in landing his first client. Most big-time athletes in one of the major sports will naturally look to someone with a track record before signing on, and few of them were likely to be won over by Barnes's list of abstract painters. So he reached down to where athletes didn't typically receive representation of any kind. He determined what the top three growth sports would be in the decade ahead—mountain biking, in-line skating, and snow boarding—then he went out and signed the top competitors in those fields, which he essentially had to himself. The contracts were small—a few thousand dollars, here and there, from compass makers, outerwear manufacturers, nutritional supplementers—which meant that his commissions were even smaller, but Barnes recognized that this was a business of relationships, and that he needed to start somewhere. He knew, for example, that the X-Games, the annual extreme sporting event staged and presented by ESPN, were the most watched athletic competition among young males aged twelve to twenty-four, bigger than the Super Bowl. He knew the money would come.

Now, with these home run balls, he saw the chance to take his start-up agency to the next level. The balls had almost nothing to do with the business plan he kept in the back of his mind—whoever heard of representing inanimate objects, like baseballs?—but he was fluid enough in his thinking to change course.

The glass wall on one side of Barnes's small ground floor office overlooked the faux-lush lobby of his building, and when he arrived that Wednesday morning, he twirled the blinds shut and started making some calls. The sign on the door said Creative Properties Management Group, and the title on his business card said Managing Partner, but really it was just Barnes, a part-time secretary, a fax machine, and a single phone line. His bookshelves told the story of his efforts to get an edge: *The Power of Nice*, *Winning with Integrity*, *Are You Paid What You're Worth?*, and *Guerilla Marketing Attacks for Attorneys*.

Barnes, a creature of nervous habit, twisted paper clips and paced the floor as he tried to track down Grass on the telephone. The cord on his phone was nearly long enough to allow him to pace all three hundred square feet of his office. When he finally reached Grass at work, he told him what a nice catch he'd made, and how happy he was to see someone hold onto one of these home run balls. Barnes tried to appeal to Grass as a baseball fan, as a fellow St. Louis native completely caught up in McGwire's magical season, as a lower middle-class guy who could definitely see the impact a ball like this could have on someone's financial situation.

Then he gave him his pitch. He was a sports agent, Barnes said, figuring he would leave out the part about representing fine artists until later. His clients included Jeff King, the three-time Iditarod champion, and Eddie

Matzger, a winner of in-line skating's 1998 World Challenge. He pointed out that these were heavy duty guys in their respective fields. Through his various contacts, Barnes suggested he was in a position to help John Grass sell the 63rd home run ball and to explore other marketing opportunities, such as endorsement and licensing deals. He explained how it was customary for sports agents to take as much as 20 percent on endorsement and licensing contracts, and anywhere from three to 10 percent on team contracts, depending on the guidelines put out by the players' association. He walked him through what some of the opportunities might look like.

Maybe we should get together, Barnes suggested, see if there might be a good fit.

The conversation had gone well, but Barnes wasn't about to wait for Grass to call him back, so he called every day until Grass finally agreed to meet with him and sign on as a client. In the meantime, McGwire and Sosa continued to hit record home runs, and because of Grass's controversial holdout, it was no longer a given that the balls would find their way back to the sluggers in trade. The way was cleared for others to sell their balls to the highest bidder, without fear of hate mail or threatening phone calls.

In the last two weeks of the season, Barnes went to work cornering the market he helped to create, and in the end secured relationships with every record home run ball that was not traded back to McGwire or Sosa:

- McGwire's 64th home run, hit September 18 in Milwaukee County Stadium, and caught by Jason King, twenty-two, of

Madison, Wisconsin, a recent graduate of Chicago State University.

- Sosa's 64th, hit September 23, also in Milwaukee, and caught by lifelong Cubs fan Vern Kuhlemeier, thirty-four, a Kelly Tire assembly line worker from Dakota, Illinois, who took his grandmother to the game to help take her mind off the death of her husband several weeks earlier.

- Sosa's 66th, hit September 25 in the Houston Astrodome, caught by tire salesman Albert Chapa, thirty-one, of Pearland, Texas.

- McGwire's 67th, hit in the fourth inning on September 26, caught by Doug Singer, thirty, a financial planner and part-time umpire from Grapevine, Texas.

- McGwire's 68th, hit three innings later, caught by twenty-five-year-old veterinary student Heath Wiseman, who flew into town from Ames, Iowa for a friend's bachelor party. Wiseman noted that he took heat from the 20 or so guys in his group for bringing his glove to the game, although it sure came in handy.

For all his extra efforts, there was nothing Barnes could do about the out-of-circulation balls. McGwire's 65th and 66th were traded back to the slugger, and Sosa's 65th was with the Cubs, after nearly being handed to that small boy outside the Astrodome by Major League Baseball's Ruben Puente. Still, with one game to go in the schedule, Barnes was well positioned to make a name for himself—and a run at the kind of money he didn't typically see in fine art or extreme sports. He felt he had a good handle on what these balls might be worth, based on what similar items had gone for in seasons past, although he recognized that buyers would likely pay a premium for the ball that stood as the ultimate record. Already, there was that much-publicized offer of $1 million for the last home run ball, from a three-headed team of collectors, and he had to think he'd be able to push that number higher, once the season was over.

For the time being, however, there was nothing to do but wait.

Four

A Pretty Good Day in the Life of a Research Scientist

September 27, 1998

As dilemmas go, this one's not much: Mark McGwire, last game of the season, at 68 home runs and counting, or the going-nowhere-fast St. Louis Rams facing the going-no-where-just-yet Arizona Cardinals, in town for the first time since the team quit their long-suffering supporters for the sweetheart leases of Phoenix. For a baseball fan, it is no contest. Even for a football fan, it's a toss-up.

The conflict didn't exactly sneak up on Philip Ozersky,

a twenty-six-year-old research scientist earning $29,000 as a finisher in the genetics lab of the Genome Sequencing Center on the Washington University campus. His colleagues had arranged for these tickets months earlier, long before McGwire shattered the home run record, and long before Rams season ticket holders were inclined to check the football schedule. The idea was to get the people from work together for an end-of-summer office party, with husbands and wives and significant others helping to fill the hundred or so bleacher and standing-room seats in the private Batting Cage party box in the left field stands. Ozersky, a big time baseball fan, was all for it. His former boss, Nancy Miller, arranged for the seats back in May (at $45 per), and she settled on the final game by default. There weren't many dates still available and the last game seemed fine, even though the Cardinals weren't likely to be in the hunt for much.

Ozersky shares his season seats to the Rams with his father, Herbert, a retired site analyst for a pharmaceutical company; his brother, David, a computer analyst, and his sister-in-law, Kristen, also have tickets, and they usually drive out to the stadium together. Between them, it's not like they couldn't find someone to take the extra ticket. In weighing which game to attend, Ozersky didn't pay much attention to whether McGwire would hit one out and set a new record. Mostly he was thinking how he and these end-of-summer lab outings at Busch had a history. Last year, he met his girlfriend Amanda Abbott in the same Batting Cage party box, so there was a little bit of a good luck thing in his thinking as well.

This game hasn't even started yet, and already he's ahead. He's here with Abbott, and a group of people have arrived early to watch batting practice and get started on the free beers—one of the bonus features of the Batting Cage party box. Ozersky, a one-time high school defensive lineman with a hangdog expression, a hands-in-pockets demeanor, and a birthmark around his left eye that leaves people wondering what happened to the other guy, is not even thinking what it would take for a ball to find its way through the giant break in the front wall of the box, opening out to a gorgeous view of the field. Most times, he goes to a game, he checks out his seats, he does a little figuring on his chances of catching a foul ball, or a home run, depending. He's been going to games all his life, a couple hundred by his count, and he's never come close. Well, once, during the 1996 Division Series against the Padres, he got his hands on a ball tossed into the bleachers by Brian Jordan, but it bounced out of his reach, and he tended not to count that one anyway because it wasn't a game ball. It was just a ball.

Here, boxed into this room, he doesn't even process his chances. It's not an impossibility, mind you, but the ball would have to come in low, at an angle, and the likelihood of a ball being hit that hard, that far, at just that right angle wasn't worth considering. However, at the very moment of Ozersky's not considering, Ron Gant sends a batting practice pitch over the left field fence and directly through the open wall of the room. Man! Ozersky keeps his eyes on the ball as it arcs towards him, but he doesn't move for it. The ball clambers up the room's portable metal bleachers and comes to rest a couple yards from where Ozersky sits. He's the first to spot it, primarily because the few people in the room aren't paying full attention. It's just batting practice, after all, and the ball comes to rest beneath the seat of Laura Courtney, a colleague in the finishing lab with what Ozersky guesses is only a passing interest in baseball.

So what does Ozersky do? He picks up the ball and hands it to Courtney. She'd have had it, easy, if she'd thought to look, and he gives it to her like this sort of thing happens every day.

For home plate umpire Richard Rieker, finishing up his fifth season in the bigs, it is a day to not screw up. After six months on the road, not seeing his family, not getting any time off more than a couple days running, not always knowing what city it is outside your hotel window, it is like a whole bag of Fridays bunched into one. It is the last day of the season, and he's thinking, *Let's bring it on. Let's get it over with and get home.*

Rieker had known for a couple days he'd be working the plate for this final game; he'd seen that was how the rotation was headed, but he didn't give it much thought. There's only so much you can pay attention to the rotation, this time of year. His main concern, when he thinks about it at all, is for the game to go smoothly. That's what people don't realize about umpiring. When you're behind the plate, or even when you're out on the bases, the thing is to call the game without incident, and in a game like this that would be especially so. History is fine, home run records are fine, but the key is for everything to come out the way it's meant. Keep your name out of the papers. You don't want to be remembered as the guy who screwed things up.

Normally, two clubs under .500, no sweat, you're playing out the string. A game like this, you'll usually see a lot of rookies, up from the minors to show what they can do, so for them it's everything. There are whole careers at stake, even though the season is shot. But here Rieker knows the baseball world will be watching. Heck, it's almost bigger than baseball, this McGwire assault. It's front-page news, all over the planet. In some ways, it's bigger than baseball needs, if such a thing is possible. See, baseball itself had plenty going on. There were, what, four National League series that meant something that final weekend. You had the Cubs, the Giants, and the Mets all going for the wild card. Going into the weekend you also had the Padres and the Astros playing for home field advantage. How often does that happen, last couple days of the season, so much on the line?

But mostly, Rieker knows, there is McGwire. It's the biggest thing he'd ever seen in baseball, this home run race. Five years is not an especially long term of service for a big league umpire, but he'd logged another dozen in the minors. He'd seen a lot of ball, and he can tell you how big this thing was. He'd drive around his neighborhood in St. Louis and see a local church with its sign out front, talking about when services were that week, when they were having their annual fish fry, and then, at the bottom, it said, "God bless you, Mark." That's how much McGwire means to the people in St. Louis, how much he means to baseball. It's bigger than sports. People who don't know a thing about the game know about McGwire. His appeal cuts across economic lines, racial lines, religious lines, every line you could imagine. You can't turn on the radio and *not* come across his name. The last thing Rieker wants is to get in the way of any of that. An umpire's job is to maintain a perfect environment for the players.

People tend to shine over events in their minds. They

forget. They forget the game in Milwaukee, just last week, fifth inning, McGwire hits a rope off pitcher Rod Henderson toward the seats in left center and some fan reaches over the railing to grab the ball and umpire Bob Davidson rules it a double. Okay, so they remember the game, Rieker supposes, but they don't think what it means from the umpire's perspective. It doesn't register that way. Happens all the time, an ump maybe misses a call, but never under this kind of microscope. McGwire's rounding the bases and Davidson actually has to send him back to second, and the crowd starts booing like crazy. The press starts calling it the 65½ home run ball. They said he should have had 66, and then Sosa went and hit his 66th and jumped out ahead. The folks around here were just about ready to string up Bob Davidson, they were so upset about the call. For a beat or two, that's how it looked, at least until McGwire hit a couple more and surged ahead, and even then there was talk of an asterisk.

Rieker had seen all the replays, and there wasn't one that showed that Davidson missed the call. There was even a shot, clear as day, front page of *USA Today*, showed the ball in the fan's glove, way over the yellow line of the fence. It was a double fence, two and a half feet separating the fans from the field of play, but a grown man, leaning over, his glove arm outstretched, he can reach over two and a half feet like nothing at all. Try it sometime and you'll see.

What happened, Rieker theorizes, was that this whole home run thing had gotten into people's guts from day one. You had a season's worth of buildup, and the fans started to see things with their hearts and not with their eyes. They wanted it to be a home run, so that's what they saw. The sportscasters, too. They've got their own emotions getting in the way, same as the fans. They're thinking about ratings, or whatever it is those people think about. Plus, you never really get the right camera angle. The only people in that ballpark who had the right angle on that call were the second base umpire and the center fielder, Grissom. They're the only ones looking straight on at the ball, and Grissom himself had come out and said Davidson made the right call.

Then there's the game he had worked about a month before, August 29 in St. Louis, Cards against the Braves, when Sam Holbrook had to toss McGwire for arguing a called third strike, and the fans were about ready to run Holbrook out of town. Can you imagine? To have to take the bat out of a guy's hands when he's chasing down a record big as this? If you want to know the truth, to Rieker's thinking, his colleague was more patient than Rieker would have been. He gave McGwire at least three warnings. Rieker himself will give a guy one warning, and if he keeps it up then he's gone. But Holbrook finally had to toss him, LaRussa and third base coach Rene Lachemann too, and the fans, they just went crazy. They threw so much garbage down onto the field it looked for a while like the Cards might have to forfeit the game. Rieker had his wife and children at the ballpark that day, and it was so bad he had the security people take them down from their seats and set them up in the umpire's room for the rest of the game.

No, it wasn't a good day to be an umpire that day against the Braves, not in St. Louis, and the last thing Rieker wanted, going into this final game, was a repeat of that kind of situation. Folks don't realize, all he has to do is call McGwire out on strikes, and if somehow Sammy Sosa winds up winning the home run race, Rieker can look out his window the next morning and find a cross burning on his front lawn. Right here in St. Louis. And God forbid he has to toss McGwire. He doesn't even want to think about that.

Rieker has enough to worry about, calling the game, and on top of that, he has to keep his "traders" straight with the ball boy, "Urkel." The system they've come up with for authenticating the balls means Rieker has to make sure he puts the correct ball in play, the one that corresponds to the chart the Major League Baseball security people are keeping over in the owner's box, behind the plate. They've got the balls marked, in sequence, and then they've got another marking on it you can only see with a special light. The numbers, though, those you can see, and McGwire will come up, the ball boy will run out four new balls, and Rieker will have to place them in order in the ball bags at his hips. He works with two balls bags, so what he'll do is empty the bags of all the ordinary balls and give them back to the ball boy. Then, he'll hold out the lowest-numbered ball for the pitcher, and put the highest-numbered ball in his left ball bag. He'll put the others in the bag on his right hip, and if McGwire fouls one off, or if the pitcher doesn't like the look of the ball he's been given, Rieker can just reach into his right bag and have a 50-50 chance on picking the next one.

He tries to commit the routine to the place in his memory where he won't have to think about it. He works through all the ways he might screw up, and he comes up nearly empty. About the only way he can think of is if McGwire hits a long foul, right down the line, just outside the foul pole, and then, the very next pitch, he hits one in almost exactly the same spot, just inside the foul pole for a home run. If he somehow puts the wrong ball into play, that's the one hole in the system. There'd be two balls out there, in virtually the same section, and it's possible someone could question which was the home run ball and which was the foul ball. It's possible the same guy could come up with both balls, and then where would we be? It isn't likely to happen, but for Rieker it is the ultimate nightmare.

Middle of the third, two outs, bases empty. Cardinals ball boy Kevin Corbin, a twenty-year-old junior at St. Louis University, puts the game on pause.

Really.

He's been doing this, last month or so, every time McGwire bats at home, and he doesn't think he'll ever lose the thrill he feels in running out these special balls to the home plate umpire. He remembers the first time—September 4, beginning of a weekend series with the Reds, the day before McGwire hit his 60th. Ever since, he's worked these moments so many times in his head that when they come around in the lineup he can almost do what he needs to do without thinking about it.

What he needs to do is this: run over to the owner's box behind home plate, where Major League Baseball's Al Williams and Linda Pantell are sitting in the aisle on folding chairs snatched from the locker room. Corbin collects from them four numbered balls, in sequence, and stops to check the stamped numbers on the balls. He has to hand the balls to the umps in order, so he puts the two lowest numbered balls in his right hand, the two highest in his left hand, and runs them out to Mr. Rieker behind home plate. Some of the umps want the balls lowest to highest, some want them highest to lowest, and this is the best way he can think to keep them straight.

After each at bat, Corbin reclaims the balls and returns them to Pantell. If it's a ground out to end the inning, he'll get the ball from the other team's first baseman. If the Cardinals are still up, and the ball is returned to the pitcher, the home plate umpire will signal for it, and Corbin'll run out and make the switch. On the way back to the owner's box, he'll look at the balls and see if they can be used again, next time up. Usually, with McGwire, he hits the balls so hard they don't come back. Either it leaves the field of play, a home run or a foul ball, or it's scuffed so badly it's out of the rotation. However it goes, it's the end of the ball.

Corbin's been a ball boy for five seasons, longer than most. It's a job he was lucky to land, back in high school, and he's not giving it up any time soon. He doesn't even mind that they all call him Urkel. First time it happened, his first year with the club, the Pirates were in town, and they had the television tuned to that show, *Family Matters*. He walked in to the visitors' clubhouse, the Pirates looked at Corbin, then they looked at the television, then the name stuck. Corbin himself can see the resemblance, although the two don't dress alike. The resemblance ends there. Now it's gotten so they all know him as Urkel. The umps, the clubhouse guys, the players. Even some of the visiting players remember him by name, one road trip to the next, and he answers to it, same way he answers to Kevin. It's all part of the same ride.

This season, most of all, it's been something he'll never forget. He tells people he has the best seat in the house, to one of the best shows in baseball history. He runs out those special balls and takes his usual post, on a stool about one hundred feet behind home plate, and then he just sits and watches, like everyone else. It's like being on the inside of a dream, looking out. He can't really describe it. He told a friend of his one time that it was like a kind of heaven. He and Tim Forneris, the guy who caught number 62, they talk about this. They even talked about it before McGwire broke the record, and he remembers Tim saying if he caught one of these balls he would definitely give it back, so he was good to his word. It gets to Corbin, at the end of the day, how connected he is to something as big as this, how close. Sometimes, McGwire'll round the bases, and Corbin'll step to home plate to switch balls with the ump, and he'll have a chance to give McGwire one of those high-fives. He's in on the celebration. He's even been in the newspaper, a couple times, and he's always on television.

No sir, he wouldn't trade seats with anyone.

Kerry Woodson sees it coming, the whole way.

There's a *crack,* and then a kind of *whoosh,* and then everyone in section 282 is on their feet, certain the ball is heading in their direction. That's how it gets, out here in these home run seats. It's a tricky angle. The ball's hit, and your stomach drops. If you're an outfielder, Woodson supposes, this is something you get used to, but if you're a fan, all the way out here, every fly ball looks like it's got your name on it.

This one, in Woodson's case, does. He reaches up and makes the grab, and his first thought, amazingly, is for McGwire. He qualifies it with a word like *amazingly* because people have since told him that their first thoughts would have centered around what the ball was worth, but Woodson's not thinking about money. He's twenty-two, freshly graduated from Southwest Missouri State, a marketing representative for his father's auto body store, and money is just not the most important thing in a situation like this. Going happily crazy and pumping his fists are the most important things. Also, thinking what an accomplishment like 69 home runs means for a guy like McGwire, and for the game of baseball. It's Ruthian. That's the word that comes to mind. It's positively Ruthian.

His second thought, also amazingly, is for Steve Ryan, the Chicago-based memorabilia dealer who teamed with New York speculators Mark Lewis and Scott Goodman to place the $1 million bounty on the last home run ball of the season. He qualifies his thinking here because just last week, on a visit to Chicago, Woodson took in a game at Wrigley and sat behind Ryan in the bleachers. Woodson mentioned that he was planning to attend the last game of the season at Busch, and Ryan told him to keep him in mind, in case he got his hands on a McGwire home run ball. He even gave the kid his business card. You never know, he said.

Naturally, the $1 million flashes through his mind—not just the amount, but the extraordinary coincidence. He starts to think maybe it was preordained, him coming up with the ball. There's a *Time* magazine reporter sitting in his section, and all game long he's been talking about the money, and soon enough Woodson's thoughts are completely routed in this direction. He's hurriedly escorted from his seat by members of Kevin Hallinan's extraction team, and as he goes, he starts to think, there's no way Felipe Alou is even gonna pitch to McGwire, rest of the game. Woodson begins to believe this so deeply, he almost wills it so. There's no way Alou is gonna let this guy beat him deep, two times in the same game, two games in a row. Not with everything Woodson's heard about Alou, how competitive he is.

He's thinking, Steve Ryan, get your $1 million ready.

Seventh inning, four or five beers in, last call.

When Philip Ozersky is not thinking about McGwire's 69th, which was incredible, or Gant's batting practice home run, which was unbelievable, he's thinking about the beer. That's pretty much the best thing about this party box, on a game-in, game-out basis. You can't always count on baseball history, and you can't always count on catching batting practice home runs, but you can count on plenty of food and drink.

It's not any kind of luxury box, this room. There are metal bleachers, a couple faded pictures dotting the spare walls, squeezed mustard packs flattened to the poured-concrete floor. There's a shot of the 1967 world championship Cardinals team, a picture of Ozzie Smith, a portrait of Red Schoendienst. Really, there's not much in the way of decoration, or direct sunlight, but when the beer flows this freely no one's complaining. No one's doing much of anything. In fact, when McGwire hauls his Bunyan-like forearms out to the plate for what will likely be his last at-bat of the season, no one is doing much of anything but watching. It gets that way, when McGwire hits—basically all the time, but lately most of all. You could be loading up on beers before they shut you off, but you'll set them down and stop to look at what will happen next, because when Mark McGwire comes to bat almost anything can happen next, and of all the things that could possibly happen next your being shut out of your last couple drafts does not tally too high on your list when weighed against most other game-related outcomes.

Still, some of Ozersky's colleagues mill about the beer stand, and some wander back to the sixteen-wheeler-sized opening atop the BJC Health Services sign with a beer in each hand, or maybe a beer and a hot dog, and they stand, riveted. People have been doing this all season. Even in batting practice, McGwire's opponents stop to watch him hit, their mouths dropped to where you could fit a baseball inside. Each turn at bat is like a scene from that old television show *Bewitched*, where Elizabeth Montgomery twinkles her nose and freeze-frames the rest of the room so that she can work her magic undetected; only here the rest of the room is Busch Stadium, and the 46,110 fans in paid attendance don't need any kind of witchcraft. They're fixed on whatever next piece of magic there might be, on their own. They are dressed mostly in Cardinal red, and they are ready for anything, and everything, all at once.

Ozersky, at least, has his hands free, and when McGwire finally sends his threshold-establishing home run toward the left field fence, the young research scientist instinctively rises to meet it. In the rising, he gets that thrilling stomach drop even major league outfielders admit to feeling when they see the ball coming their way. It is a sensation anyone who has played any kind of ball knows firsthand—that delicious, purposeful moment, tinged with fear, during which the game takes every conceivable turn in your head. It's a feeling that almost leaves a taste in your mouth. Ozersky recognizes that taste, and his heart quickens in response. His stomach's in his throat, and he's thinking, *Here it comes, here it comes, here it comes.*

A guy like Ozersky, he's always prided himself on his drive. His athletic ability, he'll admit, is right in the middle of the curve, he's never been the best at anything, but he'll run a mile to make a play. He still plays intramural softball, football, and even co-ed basketball, and the people he plays with know this about him, and it's important to Ozersky that they know this about him. He'll never fulfill the highlight-reel fantasies of his childhood, but he doesn't care if he ends up on the ground, hurt, as long as he makes the play. He's not jumping into any pool, not knowing if there's any water in it, but that doesn't mean he's not going to hurt himself, playing all out like he does, all the time.

Here, the ball reaches the small room like it has someplace else to be. It ricochets off the back wall, about twenty feet in, and Ozersky is quick enough to feel thankful he didn't try to bare-hand it and that it didn't hit him in the head. Some guy actually does reach his hand in the way of the ball, he'll see it later on the replays, and the ball changes direction a little bit, but not so much that most people notice. Ozersky notices, but at first he thinks maybe the ball hit the handrail, maybe it came in kind of low. Then he turns along with everyone else and follows its path to the wall. The people scattered among those metal bleachers turn their heads mighty quick. *Zip,* the ball whooshes past, and their heads dart as if they are all seated center court at a tennis match.

For a ball that had left Mark McGwire's bat less than five seconds earlier, Ozersky has had an enormous amount of time to think things through. Others in the box will report the same thing—that these next moments play out on a too-slow speed, all around—but it is Ozersky who uses his next moments to advantage. When the others turn to the wall, thinking perhaps the ball will have imbedded itself in the concrete, Ozersky thinks to play the carom. He works the angles in his head. He makes a quarter turn and thinks, *Okay, where's it going?* He reacts like a pool shark, and then he shifts to poker. Without really thinking about it, it occurs to him that the eyes of his colleagues will be the tell, and he quickly scans the room for someone who might have seen something or felt the breeze of the caromed ball as it bounced off the wall in front of them. What he can't see himself he can perhaps pick up on, from someone else. He inventories his friends and colleagues for a contrary expression, and he finally, miraculously spots one—on the metal bleachers, back a bit toward the wall. In an instant, he susses that what this person is looking at is slightly different than what everyone else is looking at. There might as well be a sign over this guy's head, the way his expression stands out from everyone else's. There's definitely something else going on in this person's sightline, and Ozersky follows the gaze to the floor, and there it is: Mark McGwire's 70th home run ball, resting wondrously beneath one of the thin metal slats of bleacher.

If he is anything else, as an athlete, Phil Ozersky is a football player. He may be a huge baseball *fan,* but the only game he ever truly had was football. In high school, he played offensive guard and defensive tackle, even though he was somewhat small for those positions. On the other side of the line, they were 250 pounds, 280, but Ozersky outplayed them at 180. He played every down with the kind of fearless abandon that wins football games—the same fearless abandon, it turns out, that comes in handy chasing down errant home run balls. He dives toward the ball—actually dives, the way you might have seen Ozzie Smith move to his left to grab a low liner up the middle. He doesn't care about the metal bleachers in his path, the dislocated shoulder he's nursing. He just goes for it, and on his way he has time to think how in football it's rarely the first person on a loose ball who winds up with it. They're usually trying to run with the ball or advance it in some way, or they're trying too hard and can't find the handle. Invariably, they make some kind of mistake, and the ball bounces away and into some other set of surer hands. He actually has time to think about this, as he leaves his feet and hurtles himself in the direction of the metal slats to retrieve the ball, and when he lands with a thud on his hurt shoulder, it's still foremost in his mind. He hits his elbow, hard, against the edge of one of the metal footrests but manages to reach his hand underneath the bleachers and swallow the ball in his grip. The phrase that occurs to him is *encompassing* the ball. As he does so, he notices another colleague from the lab, a young man named Jason Kramer, splayed out in a similarly awkward and reckless position, coming up just short in his reach: one beat ahead and two inches short. Ozersky considers that if there were another inch to Jason Kramer's wingspan, he might have encompassed the ball ahead of him. Ozersky looks into Kramer's eyes and gets back what he can best describe as delirium. Ozersky's own expression seems to want to explode in disbelief. He's not sure if he's speaking, or if maybe his thoughts are simply careening about in his head, but what he's thinking, and what he's thinking about saying, is *Oh, my God. Oh, my God. Oh, my God.* Over and over.

What strikes home plate umpire Rieker is the sheer velocity with which the ball leaves the park. He works close to the ground, on his knees, much lower than most guys tend to work the plate, and by the time he's shot to his feet the ball is gone.

To Rieker, it looks at first like McGwire lashes a screaming line drive back to the third baseman, only it's a line drive that somehow keeps screaming all the way to the fence. It's not clear it'll go the distance when it's hit; it's more likely it will bore a hole through the left field wall, but it just keeps going, climbing. He wonders if maybe there was some rise to it, if such a thing is possible. Anyway, it's like a bullet, is how it is, and Rieker has to think that part of what propels that bullet is all the pressure that's been heaped on Mark McGwire, all season long. When you're in the zone like that, when there's commotion all around and you're able somehow to make it fall away, it all adds up. It's got to come out somewhere, that pressure.

From this moment on, he'll be known as the ump behind the plate when McGwire hit his milestone 70th home run, but what Rieker takes away will come down to this one image of himself, hurrying to rise from his crouch before the ball clears the fence. It's like a race, him against the ball. He'll remember the game itself, and the crowd. He'll remember the grace of Mark McGwire and Sammy Sosa, the class. He'll remember the reporters and the flashbulbs. He'll remember the butterflies he felt, seven innings back, at calling a good game. But mostly he'll remember the raw power of this final swing, the hurry the ball is in. The race, as McGwire uncoiled, to have to uncoil himself in the same time it took for the ball to leave the park. To his dying day, he'll hear the number 70, and this is what he'll remember.

* * *

Right away, Ozersky is ushered into the bowels of Busch Stadium by two uniformed officers from the St. Louis Metropolitan Police Department, Ron Fiala and Rick Severino. Okay, it's not quite the bowels of the stadium, but they are certainly bound for parts unknown to a nothing-special fan like Ozersky. And it's not quite right away, but soon enough. In between, Ozersky finds time to backslap a couple friends, to show the ball around, to smile at his unlikely good fortune. He's not sure which piece of what's happened is harder to believe, that Mark McGwire actually managed to hit 70 home runs in a single season—70!—or that he, Philip Ozersky, actually managed to come up with the ball. There's no time to process what it all means. There's time for people to pour beer on him, which Ozersky later supposes is owing to the fact that it's free, but there's no time to think things through.

Also, there's no time for these cops to have been dispatched to the scene so swiftly. How did that happen? McGwire finishes rounding the bases and it's like they're already in the party box, telling Ozersky to come with them. Fiala and Severino are two of about thirty officers assigned to the stadium, most of them stationed in the left field stands. Before the game, many of these same officers worked a scalping detail outside the stadium, plain clothes, and then they put on their uniforms and shifted inside, where their mission became to get to the baseball as soon as they could. Here, in the seventh, they see the ball drop into the Batting Cage and immediately give chase. They hop over a couple sections like they're running down a perp and start banging on the door to the private room. No one opens the door, at first. There's another way in, for the concession guys, but they're pounding on this one door. At one point, Severino starts hollering, "Open up, it's the police!" like he's on some cop show, and finally they are let inside.

Sure enough, they're the first cops on the scene. Ozersky is at the center of a small cluster of people, and everyone is taking turns pouring beer on him and clapping him on the back. He's clutching so tight to the ball it might hold a secret formula for world peace. There's even another set of hands around Ozersky's, belonging to a colleague from the lab named Chris Bauer, and there's no way this ball is going anywhere. Still, Severino thinks it's a good thing they're here, because who knows what might happen. He takes one look at Ozersky and calls for a medic. He sees the birthmark under his eye and thinks the ball maybe cracked him in the face, or maybe he took a punch from someone who wanted the ball a little too much.

The two cops hurry Ozersky through his congratulations and beer dousings and escort him and his girlfriend to the KMOX interview room. That's the gauntlet they've been told to have him run, only the KMOX booth is behind home plate, half way around the stadium. They run the whole distance and at the other end of it Fiala is thinking, *Good Lord*. He can't remember the last time he ran this hard, and the worst of it is, the entire way around, people can hear them coming. It's not like it's just them, running; it's like a stampede, the running of the bulls, and people are spilling out of their seats and running alongside and trying to slap Ozersky on the back and get a look at the ball.

Just yesterday, Fiala was with the guy who caught number 67, Doug Singer, the kid from Texas, and Fiala gave him a good hard time. Singer was like most of these guys in that he was concerned about making it safely to his car with the ball, so on the way out of the stadium Fiala told Singer to let him carry it for him. "They're not gonna take it from me," he said, and he put the ball in his pocket and walked Singer to his car. When they got to the car Fiala said, "Okay, that's it then, have a good night," and he started to walk off. Singer's face just about twisted off his skull in confusion. "You still have my ball!" he shouted, and Fiala had to laugh.

With Ozersky, though, it's a little more frantic, a little more intense. Fiala and Severino keep telling him to carry the ball low, and close to his body, but Ozersky keeps holding it up where someone can grab it. Fiala thinks, *This is not good.*

When the Rams game breaks, and the Trans World Dome crowd spills out onto Broadway, it's possible to sense the excitement at Busch Stadium, a couple blocks down. Herbert Ozersky leaves the stadium with his son David and daughter-in-law Kristen, and Rudy Nissenboin, the kid next door who was only too happy to take Philip's ticket, and he can tell there's something *off* about the scene. The tailgaters have their radios on, they're honking their horns, there's definitely something doing.

But what?

It takes the Ozerskys a bit to load up the car, ever since Herb suffered a stroke in 1986, which left him paralyzed on his left side. It slows him down some, but it doesn't keep him from his beloved Rams. First it was his beloved Cardinals, the football Cardinals, but he forgot about them the day they skipped town. Now it's his beloved Rams. It's just an extra effort, is all, since the stroke, and they slowly bundle into the car and turn on the radio to determine the source of the buzz. Rudy wants to know the score of the baseball game, so they tune in to KMOX. There's Jack Buck, coming in through the speakers, talking to some kid about catching another home run ball, and immediately they get that McGwire extended his record. Even a football fan like Herb Ozersky can get excited about a thing like that.

Jack Buck is telling the kid to sit down, and the kid is trying to be gracious and telling Jack Buck, "No, no, you sit down," and David Ozersky, driving the car, is the first to recognize the voice. Then he hears his brother's name. Then he wonders what his brother is doing talking to Jack Buck, telling him to sit down. There's a beat or two when nothing makes sense. Then he realizes what's happened, and he starts to pound on the steering wheel and honk the horn.

Back at Busch, Philip Ozersky finally sits down, and he gets through his interview without incident, and afterward he asks Buck if he catches many foul balls up in this booth. Buck thinks about this a moment, and then, in the legendarily dulcet tones that have provided the soundtrack to a lifetime of Ozersky's summer evenings, he says this: "Heck, no. I get the hell out of the way." Then he tells Ozersky to get what he can for the ball.

Moments later, at the postgame press conference, Ozersky and fellow ball catcher Kerry Woodson sit in the front row as Mark McGwire tells reporters he is in awe of himself—and so, clearly, are they. Both will say later that if they had a chance to meet him, and visit with him, they would have probably turned over the balls for a handshake, but McGwire is unavailable to them. They are ten feet away, and yet no closer than the other 46,108 fans, on their way home.

After the press conference, Cardinals media relations manager Steve Zesch approaches Ozersky and offers a trade: a signed bat, ball, and jersey. It's less than some of these other guys have gotten, but it's a place to start.

"I really want to hold onto it awhile," Ozersky says, completely unsure of his plans for the ball except that it would be nice to show it to his family and friends. His whole life, he doesn't even come close to a thing like this, he's not about to give it up before he has a chance to enjoy it. It's not like he has no intention of trading the ball back to McGwire—a big part of him would like to do just that—but he can't see that he has to rush his decision. "Do we have to do this now?" he wonders. He realizes he desperately wants to meet McGwire, but he doesn't see that his giving back the ball should have anything to do with it.

Zesch explains that McGwire has a flight to catch. He reminds Ozersky that it's been a long, grueling season.

"I'd love to be able to congratulate him," Ozersky says.

"Mr. McGwire does not negotiate," Zesch says, flat, cold.

Ozersky is stunned by the response. He's not negotiating. He's not even thinking clearly. He'd been drinking for seven innings; they're lucky he's speaking in coherent sentences. He turns to Amanda Abbott and expresses his frustration. "All I wanted was to shake his hand," he says.

It's late, eleven-thirty or so. Ozersky and Abbott had meant to go to her parents' house in Town and Country, Missouri, to leave the ball in her father's safe, but the night got away from them. There was that whole crowd at his parents' house, everybody calling, people they hadn't heard from in years. There was that big dinner, Chinese take-out, when it finally occurred to someone they should think about eating. And then there was all that talk about what to do with the ball, for the time being. He should definitely go to the bank, it was agreed, take out a safe deposit box, but it was a Sunday night, and the banks were all closed. The plan, initially, was to drive out to the Abbott's house and leave the ball in their safe, but neither one of them is up to it any longer. They figure it can wait until morning. There's not much can happen to the ball in one night, they reason. A guy like Ozersky, he's had baseballs in his house his whole life, and no one's ever tried to break in and steal one. He knows this is different, but he's trying not to get too crazy about it.

He kicks off his shoes and thinks about getting ready for bed, and he suddenly remembers something he has to do. Video store. *Shit!* He all but slaps himself on the forehead for letting it go this late. He's got a tape due back at Blockbuster before midnight, and he knows it'll bug him if he lets it go until tomorrow. They charge two or three dollars in late fees these days, and there's no reason he couldn't have taken care of it already. Well, okay, he realizes. Actually there is a reason, a big reason, but there's no reason he can't take care of it now, before the store closes.

"Feel like going out for a drive?" he asks Abbott.

"Now?" she shoot back. They'd just gotten in. She's tired. They'd already blown off the idea of driving out to her parents.

"The movie's due."

It's amazing to her, he's just caught this incredible baseball, everything is happening, and he's worried about a two-dollar late charge at Blockbuster. "We'll drop it off tomorrow," she says. "On the way to work."

Ozersky would rather go now. A thing like this, it'll keep him up all night, so he steps back into his shoes, grabs the video, and heads for the door. It'll just take a few minutes. Then he remembers: the ball. He doesn't want to leave Amanda alone in the house with the ball, even though he knows she'll be fine. It's the kind of thing, though, if something happened, he'd never forgive himself, so he puts the ball back in its Ziploc bag and tucks it in the glove compartment of Amanda's aqua blue Saturn SL2 before starting up the car and backing out of the driveway.

The local Blockbuster is just five miles away, across the street from the St. Louis Galleria on Brentwood Boulevard. The small lot is essentially empty, so Ozersky pulls into a spot right out front. He thinks about taking the ball inside with him, but then he thinks it'll be fine in the glove compartment. He doesn't want to have to explain why he's walking around with a baseball in a Ziploc plastic bag. He'll lock the car. He can keep an eye on it through the window. He won't be long.

Once inside the store, however, he starts to feel a little antsy. Not about leaving the ball outside, and not about taking too long, but about everything else. So much has happened, in such a short space of time, that pieces of his day seem to want to bubble forth. It's not like Ozersky, but for some reason he's busting to talk. There's no one else around, except for two clerks and a manager, getting ready to close up for the night. He's seen these people before, but he doesn't know them to talk to them. Still, he drops the video on the counter and starts in. "So," he says. "D'you guys hear about McGwire?"

"Yeah," one of the sales clerks replies. "Pretty cool."

"Yeah," says the other.

It's not clear from the sluggish response whether these people are baseball fans, or whether they're just being polite, so Ozersky presses on. He wants to get them talking, to sort through his own thoughts in an anonymous conversation. Or maybe he just wants to see how today's excitement has registered to someone with a little more distance on the situation. "On the radio," he tries, "on the way over, they were talking about whether the guy who caught it should keep the ball or give it back."

This gets them going. They'd definitely keep it, they say. They call over to the store manager, to see what she would do, and she would definitely keep it too. Ozersky collects these opinions as if they are consequential. In his head, he's a social scientist, doing field research. From the moment he grabbed the ball, the only thoughts he's heard on what he should do with it had come from people who knew him, from people with a vested interest in his decision, from people connected in one way or another to Major League Baseball. Everybody had an opinion, even a guy like Jack Buck, but these denim-uniformed Blockbuster people have the first unbiased opinions Ozersky has heard all day. They didn't know who he was. To them, he was probably just some lonely guy, breezing in at closing, wanting to beat the late fee, trying to get a conversation going.

"Anyway," one of the clerks say at one point, perhaps tiring of the conversation and wanting to go home, "it's not like we get to have a vote or anything. It's not like any of us caught the ball."

"Well," Ozersky says, not really thinking. "You're not exactly right. The ball's just outside, in the glove compartment of my car."

From the expressions on their faces, he might as well have told them he had Jimmy Hoffa's elbows in there as well. The two clerks and the manager look at Ozersky and figure him for the kind of crank they sometimes get in here, late at night. "Yeah, right," one of them says. They return their attentions to their last-minute business.

"No, really," Ozersky insists. He probably shouldn't have said anything, but now that he has he wants to make sure he doesn't come across as a nut job. He comes in here all the time, with Amanda, with his friends. He doesn't want these people pointing him out or looking at him funny. He makes his case, tells them he's not some crazy person, tells them to look at the name on his Blockbuster account, tells them it's the same name that's been on the news, all night long.

He makes his point, to where one of the sales clerks asks to see the ball. "If it's in your glove compartment," she says, not really asking, "we can all go out and take a look at it."

Ozersky is delighted to have the opportunity to redeem himself. "Sure," he says.

"Great," the girl stage-whispers to her colleagues as the four of them step out into the still night air. "This guy's gonna kill us, right here in the parking lot." Then, to Ozersky: "You're not a murderer, are you? I mean, we'd look really stupid, anybody finds out what we were doing out here."

Underneath the joke they all realize that what they're doing is not exactly the smartest thing in the world. They want to believe Ozersky, these three Blockbuster employees. They want to rub up against baseball history, against Mark McGwire, even in this several-times-removed sort of way. They want to have a story to tell. That's why they follow this guy out to the parking lot. He could be a serial killer, but they don't think so. Plus, the parking lot is pretty well lit. There are three of them and only one of him. What could happen?

Ozersky is not thinking in inverse terms. It might have occurred to him that there was only one of him and three of them, and they could have easily jumped him right there in the parking lot and made off with the ball, but at the time, all he is thinking is proving himself sane.

"Here," he says, leaning in to Abbott's car and pulling out the baggie. "Number Seventy." He hands the bag over to the female salesclerk the way a proud father might show off his kid's report card.

They make an incongruous picture, the four of them, huddling in a parking lot at midnight. From a distance, they might be trading weapons, or drugs, or stolen videos from the still-lit store.

"Wow," the girl says, staring at the ball, then back at Ozersky. "So you're the guy?"

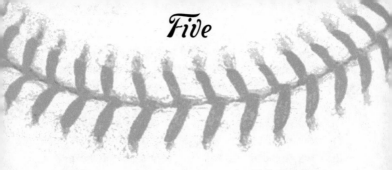

Five

Opening Bids

*Or, Bright Ideas
and Lesser Thoughts*

One of the first calls Philip Ozersky paid attention to was
from his cousin, David Krathen, a medical malpractice attorney in Fort Lauderdale, Florida. Like most everyone
else beneath the shade of the Ozersky family tree, Krathen's ears had picked up when he heard the news of
Mark McGwire's 70th home run—only he felt he could be
of some help to Philip, rather than the other way around.

Krathen knew there'd be offers to field, counsel to be
given, contracts to be negotiated. He didn't see why these
trusts should be placed outside the clan. He thought his
young cousin—actually, his wife's cousin—had enough to
worry about without worrying also whether he could
count on his advisers. He told Ozersky he'd make himself and his offices available to him, at no charge, until
Ozersky decided what he'd do with the ball. Krathen's

thinking was that a plan could be put in place and carried out in a matter of weeks, without placing too much of a burden on his practice, and even if it was too much of a burden, that would still be okay. This was family.

Michael Freedland, another cousin—actually, a second cousin, once removed—and an associate in Krathen's firm, was handed the ball, in every sense of the phrase. At twenty-six, one year out of law school, Freedland was hardly familiar with the sports collectibles market. His first-hand experience in the world of professional sports was limited to an obsessive interest in John Madden's 1997 Sony Playstation National Football League game. Freedland wasn't even a baseball fan, so his frames of reference were slightly off. Moreover, he wasn't particularly practiced as a negotiator, accustomed as he was to the orderly back-and-forth that came in personal injury and wrongful death cases. He could listen to an offer on behalf of a plaintiff, and advise whether it was too low or too high; he could tell a client if he thought he might do better at trial. Here, though, there was no good way to value his client's "claim." Everybody's best guesses, which were about all he had to go on, weren't worth the saliva needed to give them voice.

In the first couple days, Freedland fielded several dozen inquiries on his cousin's behalf, and it was quickly apparent that this McGwire ball wasn't like any other baseball to ever reach the open market. And why limit it to baseballs? It was unlike any artifact the game had known. This was a Honus Wagner card, in pristine condition, times two. That's the kind of money that seemed to be out there, judging from these early calls. He got the Wagner reference with a little research. He learned that when hockey great Wayne Gretzky and pre-convict Bruce

McNall purchased a T-206 tobacco card of Pittsburgh Pirates Hall of Fame shortstop Honus Wagner at a 1991 Sotheby's auction for $451,000, the news was reported on the front page of every newspaper in the country. When the card was resold a few years later, this time for $641,000, it made headlines all over again, and from what he was hearing his cousin's ball was likely to eclipse those amounts by a wide margin.

To begin, there was the matter of the standing $1 million offer. Actually, there were two separate $1 million offers reported in the papers, but one—a vague, anonymous proposal that was somehow meant to publicize the 1980 murder of four Americans, three nuns, and a lay worker, in El Salvador—never materialized on Freedland's call sheet. The other took a couple inquiries to reveal itself for what it was: an annuity, payable in $100,000 installments over ten years, with no guarantees. It was a considerable sum, but it was not quite $1 million. In present value, it represented about $200,000 to $350,000—again, a lot, but not quite what the collective bargainers had in mind. The offer came from three of the biggest memorabilia dealers in the country—Mark Lewis, of Long Island; Scott Goodman, of Staten Island; and Steve Ryan, of Chicago—and they were hoping to make a preemptive strike on a private sale. Originally, they put the money up for the record-breaking home run, but when McGwire's 62nd home run ball never made it into circulation, the collectors switched gears and applied the same terms to the last home run ball of the year. They had it all figured. They'd get themselves on *Letterman* and *Good Morning America*. They'd get their names in the mainstream papers. They were known in the hobby, but their $1 million would get them noticed everywhere else, and they'd use the attention to showcase their extensive memorabilia collections, maybe even win a few choice consignments out of the publicity. Then they'd turn and sell the ball to a major corporation—a McDonald's, or a Pepsi—for two, three, maybe four million dollars.

It never occurred to Mark Lewis that the ball wouldn't wind up in his collection. "Who turns down a million dollars?" he wondered. "Who in their right mind?"

Ozersky, for one. He wasn't a seller at that price, on those terms, and the three collectors hadn't counted on that.

His very first week on the case, Freedland took a call from Scott Goodman that caught him completely by surprise. I'm rich, Goodman reportedly declared. I'm not just rich, I'm filthy rich. The kind of rich you don't know anything about. Freedland wrote everything down; he wanted to be sure to remember it all. It was his experience that anyone who went so far out of his way to tell you how much money he had probably didn't have quite as much as he said. Goodman explained how he had come into an inheritance, how all he cared about was baseball, how baseball made him happy. He wanted that ball. Just tell me what you want, he said. We'll work something out.

Freedland hung up the phone and thought, *Okay, this could be interesting.*

It was difficult for Philip Ozersky to get his hands around $1 million. It was one thing to get his hands around a baseball that might be worth as much as $1 million, but it was quite another to understand what that money might mean. Really, it was the *idea* of that kind of money that was hard to find a place for.

It carried with it an enormous responsibility. Maybe

it was the way he came to it that left Ozersky thinking the money was meant for more than him. Maybe it was the way his coming up with the 70th home run ball placed him in a kind of spotlight, left him thinking he should put the money to work in a public way, for the greater good. He kept coming back to that phrase, *the greater good*. He used it in considering whether he should donate the ball to the Hall of Fame or return it to McGwire. When he put his thoughts into words, there it was: the greater good. Mostly, he thought that if he kept control of the ball, he could direct its impact. He considered whether the enjoyment of a relative few visitors to Cooperstown outweighed the benefits his ball could bring to any number of local charities, or to any number of underprivileged children. In his day-dreamings, he kept processing things in terms of children, and he wondered how much of this had to do with McGwire. He was well aware of McGwire's efforts on behalf of abused kids—more than anything else, it was the slugger's personal cause—and Ozersky supposed it was fitting to direct his proceeds from the ball in just this way. Plus, he always liked children, and it tore at his heart, some of the stories he'd hear, what some kids were put through.

But just which kids were in need, and just how much money would Ozersky have to spread around? The more he thought about it, the more he kept raising the bar. Funneled into the right program, $10,000 would accomplish a lot, but not as much as $100,000, and $100,000 wouldn't go as far as $1 million. He wasn't used to thinking in these kinds of numbers, but now that he had landed on them, it was tough to bounce off.

He wondered how much would be enough.

* * *

When an entrepreneur like Gary Summers tells you he has a ton of one thing or another crowding his warehouse facilities, he means it. Like, oh, the Berlin Wall. He'd successfully imported and sold seventeen tons of the wall, and as of September 1998, he still had one ton left to move. And that wasn't even counting the eye-poppingly graffitied section he'd picked out for his fantasy fireplace, in the last home he intends to build. (For the mantel, he had set aside the jump board from the long jump pit at the 1996 Summer Olympic games in Atlanta, after having sold off the sand at an estimable profit.)

Summers has had a ton of ideas in his unconventional sales and marketing career, and he's seen a goodly percentage of them to fruition, like the time he bought up the turf at Texas Stadium and sold it off in chunks to die-hard Dallas Cowboy fans. When he sets his mind to a thing, he's all over it. He's the kind of guy who only takes no for an answer when you spell it out for him. In big letters. With emphasis added. He likes to tell people he falls on his face every few years, and when Mark McGwire hit his 70th home run of the season, his cheeks hit the floorboards hard. That ball was like a license to print money, Summers thought, and from what he saw on the news, the kid who caught it, Ozersky, seemed like a decent enough person. He only wanted what everyone else wanted, what Summers himself wasn't ashamed of wanting. He wanted to make a buck, and to make a difference. Good for him, Summers thought. And good for Summers, too, if he could find a way to get to Ozersky.

His first thought was to market the image of the ball in a hologram form, perhaps as a tie-in with a credit card company. It wasn't the best idea in the world, Summers would be the first to tell you, but it was the first thing he came up with. Certainly, it was good enough to bring to Ozersky, but the kid wouldn't take his calls. Summers could understand that, with what that kid must have been going through that first day, so he made one of his patented extra efforts. Like he said, he doesn't take no for an answer. He made a cold call to a local Ford dealership outside Olivette, Missouri, Ozersky's hometown. He asked to speak to the youngest, most aggressive salesman on the lot. He always said, if you want to get something done in a town where you don't know the first thing, reach out to a top car salesman. He could help you hustle your way into anything.

Summers was put in touch with a young gun named Dan Torrence, and he offered him a deal: Hand-deliver a proposal to Philip Ozersky in the next twenty-four hours, and Summers would cut him in on whatever arrangement came as a result. To an ambitious salesman like Torrence, there was nothing to lose but a few minutes of his time— and everything to gain. Summers faxed Torrence his proposal to represent and market the hologram image of the ball, and Torrence found a way to get it to Ozersky in the next hour. Don't ask Summers how the kid managed it, but he did.

The moment Mike Barnes started chasing down record home run balls was the moment his business changed. In fact, his whole life was reinvented. It used to be his days were fairly routine, his hours somewhat predictable, but now there was no telling what would come up next, or where it would take him, or what this kid Ozersky would do with his good fortune. Barnes was a kid himself, at twenty-eight, but the newspapers were all referring to Ozersky as a kid, and he had picked up on it.

He made a couple calls and was eventually routed to Ozersky's attorneys in Florida, and within a week, Barnes had arranged to fly down for a meeting. Michael Freedland picked him up at the Ft. Lauderdale airport on a round-trip, after dropping off Arlan Ettinger, the president of Guernsey's, the first auction house to make a direct appeal for Ozersky's consignment. Then the two drove back to the law offices of David Krathen, where Barnes pitched his way into the fold with his innovative ideas and enthusiastic style. He viewed the opportunity to maximize Ozersky's return on the ball as a joy and a challenge, both, and a chance to grow his own agency. That he was down in Florida at all, soliciting the business, was a good sign to Krathen and Freedland, and Barnes laid out a plan for personal appearances, endorsements, licensing and marketing opportunities, and the direct sale of the ball itself. He returned to St. Louis with an agreement to represent the ball, and its owner, in all markets. The one caveat was that Barnes would only commission monies due Ozersky on the sale of the ball above $1.25 million, which was the highest offer Freedland had fielded before Barnes joined the team; on all other deals, such as licensing and endorsements, Barnes would commission on the full amount. The $1.25 million offer came from a New York dealer named Gary Zimet, who ran an on-line auction service called Moments in Time, which featured, among other items, the record album cover John Lennon signed for Mark David Chapman on the afternoon of his assassination.

Ozersky joined John Grass (McGwire #63), Jason King

(McGwire #64), Doug Singer (McGwire #67), Heath Wiseman (McGwire #68), Kerry Woodson (McGwire #69), Vern Kuhlemeier (Sosa #64), and Albert Chapa (Sosa #66) in Barnes's unlikely stable of clients, each of whom was anxiously awaiting his unlikely windfall. In each case, Barnes cut his usual fee by as much as 50 percent, thinking there would be a dozen other agencies desperate to represent these guys. As it turned out, he was the only player, but he didn't regret what he'd given up. It was the cost of doing business, he said, a calculated risk.

From the beginning, Barnes was able to persuade his new clients to act as a group, as much as possible. It gave him a certain leverage, in negotiating with corporate sponsors, and in exploring product tie-in promotions. Plus, as soon as one ball sold, he maintained, it would establish a market for the others, so it was in everyone's best interests to sit back and allow the offers to find their natural level. Time was their friend; haste, their enemy. He dreaded the thought that one of his guys would get antsy and sell too soon, before Barnes had a chance to fully test the marketplace.

One of Freedland's initial moves on Ozersky's behalf was to assist in placing the ball on display at the St. Louis Cardinals Hall of Fame, which occupied a wing of the International Bowling Museum and Hall of Fame. Barnes was in place in time to work the follow-through. The move accomplished two things: It allowed Ozersky to share the ball with Cardinals fans like himself—and, in so doing, it allowed Barnes a base of operations. The museum, located on Stadium Plaza across the street from Busch Stadium, offered a convenient backdrop for advertisers and reporters needing access to the ball.

Ozersky's first ball-related pay day came for allowing

Professional Sports Authenticators, a leading authenticator of baseball cards and other sports memorabilia, to mark the McGwire ball with an invisible DNA trace liquid, which could be read with a special laser light. According to PSA spokesman Miles Standish, the Major League Baseball markings on Ozersky's ball would fade over time, and this would be especially so if the ball was placed under direct lighting, such as you might find in a museum display case. The DNA tag, however, would never fade, Standish said, no matter what lighting or climate conditions the ball was subjected to. In fact, the trace liquid had been tested by a jeans company in a PSA promotion and subjected to twenty-five acid washings and twenty-five stone washings, after which the tag still showed up as clear as the day it was placed.

The PSA/DNA technology was developed to validate the legitimacy of certain high-end collectible items, and the California-based company sought Ozersky as their first "celebrity" spokesman. For agreeing to use the service, in a ceremony at the Bowling Hall of Fame that for some reason involved an armored car, Ozersky received $10,000, out of which he donated $1,000 to Cardinals Care, the St. Louis Cardinals' community fund. Barnes's other clients received $1,000 for participating in the promotion.

For the most part, the calls to Barnes's office came in two forms: auction houses, looking to win Ozersky's consignment, and private bidders, looking to keep the ball from going to auction. Krathen and Freedland were so taken by Arlan Ettinger's personal presentation that they were inclined to auction the ball through Guernsey's, but they had Barnes play out their other options just the same. The calls came in bunches, several hundred in the first week alone. There was also an occasional licensing inquiry that Barnes felt worth pursuing, such as the proposal from the one-of-a-kind puzzle maker, Stave's, the New England company known for supplying premium jigsaw puzzles to First Lady Barbara Bush while she was in the White House. Stave's wanted to make seventy handcut, wooden puzzles featuring the ball, which it planned to sell for $700 apiece, with 50 percent going to Ozersky, but Freedland ultimately quashed the deal, referring to Ozersky's take as "chump change," when compared to what the ball itself might bring. This was true, Barnes allowed, but it was also true that Ozersky's $24,500 represented nearly a year's salary. It was all a matter of how you looked at it.

Undaunted, Barnes pressed ahead on another side deal. He came to an agreement with noted St. Louis baseball photographer Don Marquess to produce a limited-edition print of the 70th home run ball, complemented by a limited-edition poster run. Marquess would market seventy artist's prints, priced at $2,500 each, and seven thousand posters, at $70 each, and share half the proceeds with Ozersky. Cardinals Care would receive $500 for every print sold, and $5 for every poster; Marquess would absorb the marketing and distribution costs from his own share, which meant that Ozersky stood to earn another $297,500 in a complete sell-through. The money wasn't guaranteed, but it wasn't chump change.

Barnes made a list of the major corporations he thought might be interested in owning the ball for promotional reasons, or in hiring Ozersky for commercials or public appearances. His list included Coca-Cola, Chase

Manhattan Bank, Sprint, Kodak, Western Union, Fruit of the Loom, Morgan Stanley, and America West. He remembered the widely publicized Sotheby's sale of the bones of the Tyrannosaurus Rex dinosaur excavated in Montana some years earlier, and bought at auction in 1997 for $8.6 million by a consortium of corporate buyers that included McDonald's and Disney. That was the kind of money he was hoping to tap into here, and if the money wasn't going to be there on the direct sale of the ball, he could definitely tap some of those deep pockets for an advertising campaign. During the baseball season, for example, there had been a popular series of MasterCard commercials featuring a father and son going to a game, with a tag line comparing the price of a baseball to the value of a conversation between parent and child. Barnes was certain the MasterCard people would pounce on his new client for a spin-off spot based on the series, and he pursued them diligently.

He was also certain he could convince *Hustler* magazine publisher Larry Flynt to make a run at Kerry Woodson's 69th home run ball, for what he blushingly said were obvious reasons. He reached out to the Nintendo Corporation, on behalf of Jason Singer's 64th McGwire ball and Vern Kuhlemeier's 64th Sosa ball, hoping to tie-in to their Nintendo 64 video game system. And, he held discussions with officials at Upper Deck on behalf of all his clients, to explore a series of baseball cards featuring the record home run ball catchers.

His wife Laura complained that Barnes was hardly available to help around their busy household—in addition to their own four-year-old son, the couple also took care of an eight-year-old nephew and a six-year-old niece—and he had to agree with her. In October alone, his telephone bill was over $3,000, and his travel expenses included last-minute, full-price airplane tickets to New York, Chicago, Ft. Lauderdale, and Los Angeles. Still, a shot like this, Barnes felt he had to rise to meet it. Even at half his usual rate, he stood to make a considerable amount of money; more than the money, he stood to make a reputation. Already, he was in the papers. People were starting to notice. Even David Falk, perhaps the most successful sports agent in the field, knew who he was. David Falk! That was like telling a start-up software developer that Bill Gates was familiar with his work. The story came back to Barnes from a mutual acquaintance that when his name came up in a related conversation, Falk remarked, "I can't believe that kid had the balls to go after these guys."

That, to Barnes, was the ultimate compliment—and a sure sign he was onto something.

Sometimes a great notion is, well, not.

Jeff Becket, a Detroit-based memorabilia marketer and supplier of sports collectibles to the QVC shopping channel, didn't much care who set the home run record, only that someone did—and only that it was possible to extract a whole bunch of good-size threads from the record-setting ball. At some point in mid-August, he actually grabbed a Tony Clark autographed ball from his collection and tore the cover off of it, to see what was inside. What he saw was green.

In fact, when he pulled out the red stitching and liberated the cowhide top from the ball's core, what he saw was cotton. He unraveled the windings, and measured them, and crunched some numbers. His plan, when he adjusted his eyes to accommodate the brilliance of the idea, was to contact Rawlings and hire them to make a half million less-than-official baseballs, each containing a single thread from the record ball, which he would then sell for $29.95. Then—to ease his conscience, or silence his critics, or both—he would re-sew the original covers around a new set of windings and donate the ersatz ball to the Hall of Fame. The way he had it figured, it was a $15 million deal. He arrived at $29.95, he said, because it was a great retail price. "It's something kids can afford for themselves," he explained.

Plan B was to team with Salvino's, makers of the Bamm Beanos line of plush toys, to market a line of one million bean bag dolls, each stuffed with an original thread from the ball, and priced at $19.95—a $20 million deal, if he sold through his inventory. Here again, a new ball would be made from the covers of the old.

The key to both deals was getting his hands (and scissors) on the record ball at a reasonable price. Becket's first impulse was to blanket the outfield bleachers at the last remaining Cubs and Cardinals games with hired fans. This might have worked, but after Maris's record fell and all these well-meaning people started *giving* the balls back to McGwire, the mood in those outfield seats was a shade too philanthropic for Becket's capitalist streak. Instead, he decided to wait until the record was set, and then start making some calls.

He didn't wait long. By Monday morning, September 28, he had reached Ozersky's parents' house in Olivette, offering the kind of money that ensured a return call. Becket anticipated some resistance to his cutting-up-the-ball idea, so he dressed it up a bit for the answering machine. "I left a message saying that mine was the only proposal they'd hear that would send the ball to the Hall of Fame," he remembered. "He'd make money, I'd make money, and the ball would go to Cooperstown."

"When you think about it," he said later, "the negative reaction was just going to come from old people. Kids loved the idea. I mean, come on, if you were a kid and you had a chance to own an official baseball with a thread from Mark McGwire's 70th home run, it's like a dream come true. It's just a baseball. It doesn't mean anything. America was captivated by the home run race, and what happens in this country when we become fascinated by something? We want to own a piece of it."

If anyone complained too loudly about Becket's plans to desecrate a piece of baseball history, he explained The Ball Formerly Known as the 70th Home Run Ball concept, which would have allowed him to wrap the original cover around a whole new ball and donate it to Cooperstown. "It's the perfect solution," he insisted, although he did not take the trouble to contact the museum's curators to see if they'd be interested in displaying the tampered-with item. "It's the chance to make a lot of money, give 90 percent of the people what they really want, and satisfy the other 10 percent that you're giving something back to the game."

Becket also held out the possibility that fan and media reaction might be so intensely negative that he could simply make his profit by selling the ball to a white knight. "In that respect, it was kind of like a hostage deal," he said. "Someone could have come in and rescued the ball. It wasn't my preferred course, but it was an option."

Becket offered $1 million for the ball. Ozersky was unimpressed—both with the money and with the idea of dismantling a storied baseball artifact. Becket ultimately reached $1.5 million, but he never quite made it past Mike Barnes with a formal proposal. Soon, he could see that the other offers were putting the ball out of his reach and that his notion, to Ozersky, was anathema.

"In my heart, I know I was doing the right thing with this deal," Becket insisted later, after his efforts had been largely ignored. "I was the good guy. Someone was gonna come in and bastardize this ball, and it was never gonna benefit the fans. Even if it went to the Hall of Fame, how many people would go to see it in Cooperstown? When you think about it, nobody really cares what's inside the ball. They care about what they can see. They care about the story that goes with it, and the story would have been the same. You can't rewrite baseball history."

No, but you could license it, or sell it off for parts.

On the single telephone line to Mike Barnes's 300-square-foot office, it was sometimes possible to win a call-waiting battle and still lose the war. The man was on the phone constantly, and if you meant to get on it with him you had to wait in line.

Three viable possibilities began to emerge in Barnes's cauliflowered ears. The first—and possibly the most workable, according to Barnes's read on Krathen, Freedland, and Ozersky—was to take the ball to auction. For weeks, every major auction house in the country had been aggressively seeking Ozersky's consignment, and most were prepared to negotiate their commissions into the single digits, from the standard 15 percent. Already, Krathen and Freedland were sold on Arlan Ettinger and Guernsey's, a small Manhattan house perhaps best known for its successful sale of the John F. Kennedy and Jacqueline Onassis estates. Ettinger's hook was to conduct the sale at Madison Square Garden, a prospect that appealed to an avid sports fan like Ozersky.

But Barnes felt he had to at least look at some of the other auction houses—if not for Ozersky, then certainly for his other clients. The easy choices were the household names in the business, Christie's and Sotheby's, but Barnes was learning that both were no longer highly regarded for their sports auctions. The front-runner, in Barnes's estimation, had to be Mastro's Fine Sports Auctions of Chicago, run by sports memorabilia expert Bill Mastro, who at one time headed the sports collectibles department at Sotheby's. There was Leland's, also of Chicago. Too, there was the Fisher Auction Company of Pompano Beach, Florida, and its pitch was to hold the sale in Miami on Super Bowl weekend. The argument against Fisher was that they were known for their real estate and foreclosure sales, but Barnes had to give these guys points for hustle; every morning, his fax machine was crowded with their appeals and updates and modified proposals. For several days, Fisher vice president Doug Dennison had also sent copies of his open airline tickets, to show he was prepared to fly to St. Louis on a moment's notice to make a presentation.

The two other possibilities were private sales—to a comic book publisher or to a maker of plush toys modeled after the successful Ty line of Beanie Baby products. Todd McFarlane, the creator of the *Spawn* comic books, and the HBO series and feature film of the same name, expressed a strong interest in Barnes's entire inventory. McFarlane, who introduced himself to Barnes as "a baseball psycho," was a one-time low-level prospect in the Seattle Mariners organization, and a part owner of the Edmonton Oilers

National Hockey League franchise. He offered to take all eight balls off Barnes's hands for a flat $2 million, but Barnes told him to break the offer down so that it attached a specific value to each ball in the group. Clearly, he couldn't negotiate on his clients' collective behalf, when some of the balls were far more valuable than others. He also told McFarlane that the package wasn't worth nearly enough for him to bring it to his clients.

McFarlane retooled his offer and came back with the following: $1.75 million for Ozersky's ball; $350,000 for Sosa's 66th; $200,000 each for McGwire's 63rd, 64th, 67th, 68th, and 69th; and $150,000 for Sosa's 64th. The package came to $3.25 million, and Barnes ran the numbers in his head and wished he hadn't given away so much of his commission. It still wasn't enough for his clients, but at least they had something to talk about.

The other leading offer was intriguing for the way it provided Ozersky with a significant up-front payment and the chance at a significant back-end royalty. It was also intriguing for the way it seemed to ace Jeff Becket out of one of his cut-up-the-ball concepts. Mike Berkus, of Sports Marketing International, a Lynwood, Washington outfit working in cooperation with Salvino's, makers of the Bamm Beano's line of plush teddy bears, envisioned a promotion involving McGwire's 70th home run ball and Sosa's 66th home run ball. Becket claimed to have introduced the idea of doing some sort of promotion surrounding the ball to Salvino's, but here the company had a more palatable approach. Berkus opened the discussion by offering Barnes $1 million for the McGwire ball, and $250,000 for the Sosa ball, with the chance to earn additional monies based on sales of licensed McGwire and Sosa bears. The bears would then be sold with a special serial number, or an entry form, and one lucky buyer of each would win a trip for two to the 1999 All-Star game in Boston and the chance to present the record home run balls back to McGwire and Sosa in a nationally televised ceremony.

Berkus pitched it as a win-win situation, and in fact it was, provided his company could come up with a little more money up front and a guarantee on sales. He proposed a 50 cent royalty on the McGwire bears and a 25 cent royalty on the Sosa bears, but these numbers were meaningless to Barnes until he could attach sales figures to them. To Barnes's thinking, the Beanie Baby market was a trend waiting to fade, and he wasn't going to put his clients in a position where they would have to stand in line with other creditors to collect their money.

Ozersky liked the Salvino's deal for the good kharma that surrounded it. He could see the ball safely back into McGwire's hands and still make over $1 million. Way more. This guy Berkus was talking about shipping as many as 10 million bears, and at 50 cents a bear that was another $5 million. True, there were no guarantees, but there were never any guarantees, and he had been losing sleep over holding onto the ball. He didn't like going against McGwire. He didn't like getting hate e-mail. He didn't like hearing his name on KFNS in a negative context. He could rationalize his thinking all he wanted: How many people would actually *see* the ball at Cooperstown? How many people could he actually *help* with the monies the ball might generate for various charities? Talk about the greater good. . . . Five million dollars could go a long way toward helping a lot of children.

Ozersky thought that if he could maximize his return on the ball, and make a sizeable contribution to causes that were important to him and to McGwire, he could shoulder the criticism. Already, with the Don Marquess photographic prints, he had earmarked as much as $70,000 to Cardinals Care, and that was without relinquishing the ball itself. Ozersky kept coming back to the notion that there was a way to do everything he wanted with the ball and still manage to return it to McGwire. It was out there, he felt sure.

All Mike Barnes had to do was find it for him.

November 3, 1998. Acting on behalf of five friends, entertainment lawyer Larry Shire beat out an anonymous telephone bidder at Christie's East and purchased Mark McGwire's 50th home run ball of the 1998 season for $46,000.

The sale was remarkable for several reasons. It was the first of McGwire's 1998 record home run balls to be sold at auction and, therefore, established a market price for the others. It received extensive, off-the-sports-page coverage. And it marked one of the top baseball sales in history, despite the fact that it was a ball many collectors felt had little historic value.

Shire begged to differ. He saw the ball as laden with history. Among his many other accomplishments during the 1998 season, McGwire became the first player to hit 50 home runs in three consecutive seasons, breaking a record he had shared with Babe Ruth. As such, Shire's ball was a totem to a singular achievement. As a record, Shire allowed, it wasn't likely to stand (a healthy McGwire would probably hit another 50 in 1999), but the ball would always mark the *first* time a player had reached that milestone, and to Shire's thinking, it ranked right up there with some of the other prized home run balls.

The purchase was also striking with respect to Shire's plans for the ball: He didn't have any. He and his fellow investors weren't planning to put the ball on display. They weren't planning to donate it to the Hall of Fame. They weren't planning to flip it for a profit at another auction. And they certainly weren't planning to lock it away in a safe deposit box. Rather, they were simply looking to *own* a piece of baseball history, to take turns holding it, to pass it back and forth as a kind of time-share souvenir.

It was, they all thought, a cool thing to have. It was not, however, the kind of cool thing any one of them could separately afford.

The Christie's auction was itself notable for a misunderstanding regarding another item offered for sale. Lot #311, donated by St. Louis Cardinals manager Tony LaRussa, was purportedly a game-used baseball, fouled into the Cardinals dugout by McGwire during a game against the Brewers on September 8, 1998, the same game in which he hit his 64th home run. According to the auction catalogue, the ball was retrieved by LaRussa and offered for sale to benefit his Animal Rescue Foundation. Regrettably, for LaRussa and the animals he was meaning to rescue, the ball was not marked by Major League Baseball, and official records indicated that it was never pitched to McGwire during a game. It may have been a foul ball, and it may indeed have been hit during the September 8 game, but it wasn't a McGwire foul ball, and to a collector, this was a key distinction. It was the difference between, say, a $200 ball and a $2,000 ball.

Prior to the auction, LaRussa huddled with the Christie's auctioneer to clear the confusion. He had seen the catalogue and grown concerned. "That might not be a foul ball of McGwire's bat," he explained to the young woman. "If there's no number on it, it's not from McGwire's bat."

"Well," the young woman said, "we should probably announce that, don't you think?"

LaRussa said he didn't know the first thing about auctions but thought this was probably something a buyer would want to know.

Six

A Still Reasonably Good but Nevertheless Troubling Day in the Life of a Research Scientist

November 12, 1998

A theory emerges: At an auction, the money in the room exists in inverse proportion to the number of people wearing overalls and baseball caps.

Philip Ozersky and Amanda Abbott arrive at the

Phillips-Selkirk auction house in suburban Clayton, Missouri about ten minutes ahead of the first gavel. They scan the warehouse showroom, looking for Mike Barnes and hoping to not be seen. The not being seen is owing to the way Ozersky has become semifamous all over town. He's recognized in restaurants, on supermarket checkout lines, in bookstores. He doesn't mind the attention, but it unsettles him.

Scanning, Ozersky and Abbot inventory some of the items up for bid. There's a lot to look at, but not much worth having: a windup toy chicken, made in Germany; a two-piece Jordache luggage set; an apothecary balance scale. It seems more a garage sale than a "collectible and couture" auction (there are blue velvet housecoats, and wall thermometers advertising Coca-Cola and L&M cigarettes), and yet the place is filled with anxious bidders. It is filled, also, with television cameras and reporters, because hidden among the dross are two prized items— an ivory-satin, ruffled-collar bridesmaid's gown from the Royal Wedding of Princess Diana and Prince Charles, designed by David and Elizabeth Emanuel, and Mark McGwire's first home run ball of the 1998 season, an opening day grand slam off Los Angeles Dodger pitcher Ramon Martinez.

Mainly, Ozersky is here to acquaint himself with the auction scene. About the only experience he's had with auctions has come from the movies, and he figures if he's considering consigning his ball to one of the major auction houses he would do well to see what's involved. So, there's that. He's also curious to see what the action is on the McGwire ball.

Barnes is also anxious to see what kind of excitement a McGwire home run ball can generate in a live auction. In the past six weeks, he's spent so much time on the phone with auction house representatives he feels he needs a frame of reference, so that he might be better equipped to advise his clients. Christie's, Sotheby's, Guernsey's, Fisher, Phillips-Selkirk . . . these people are all talking to him like he's a veteran of these sales, when really he's got no idea. He wants to understand it, from the floor, because one of the things he's weighing is whether to seek a live auction or a mail and telephone sale, spread over two or more days. The two biggest sports auction houses in the business, Mastro's and Leland's, work almost exclusively with absentee bidders, believing it affords buyers more privacy than a live auction, and more time to contemplate their bidding. Barnes wants a basis for comparison.

First, he stops on his way in to conduct a little business. Earlier, he let slip to one of the potential buyers of Ozersky's ball, comic book publisher Todd McFarlane, that he was planning to attend the Selkirk sale, and McFarlane asked him to submit an absentee bid on his behalf. Barnes was happy to oblige, even though he himself had been thinking he might make a run at the ball. The estimated sale price on the ball, according to the catalogue, was $10,000 to $12,000, but Barnes knew it to be worth a lot more. He also knew that some items sell for substantially less than the estimate. As far as he knew, there was no minimum reserve on the ball, so there was a chance he could get it at a good price—or, at least, a price he could justify to his wife.

McFarlane, however, has been in serious pursuit of Ozersky's ball, and the other McGwire and Sosa balls in Barnes's stable, and Barnes is inclined to do whatever the guy asks. Apparently, McFarlane wants to get his hands on every ball he can and put together a kind of traveling exhibit of the home run balls of 1998 to accompany his famous "Spawnmobile" to toy shows around the country. His thinking is the attention generated by the baseballs will lift interest in his comic books and action figures, and Barnes convinces himself he can see the synergy. The ball offered at today's auction, McGwire's 1st, fit neatly into McFarlane's strategy, and he instructed Barnes to submit an anonymous "up to" bid of $50,000, which killed Barnes's interest. His pockets were not nearly so deep.

Typically, with an absentee bid, the auction house allows a client who cannot attend the sale to top the highest bid, up to a specified, preapproved amount. Barnes can't compete for the ball at McFarlane's level, so he doesn't even bother to register for a paddle. He deposits McFarlane's bid form in the Selkirk office off the lobby and moves into the showroom, where he hooks up with Ozersky and Abbott. Almost immediately, the large showroom seems to tilt on a new axis. A reporter spots Barnes and Ozersky and puts two and two together to come up with a bigger story than a dress and a grand slam ball. Headlines are rewritten on the fly: "Ball Holder and Ball Agent Attend Auction." Cameras spin on their tripods in the direction of Ozersky and Barnes. It is as if McGwire himself, and his agent, have stopped by to check out a few innings of a Little League game.

A corollary: At an auction, the number of news cameras and microphones pointed at individuals having nothing directly to do with the items being offered for sale can be used as a negative predictor of the sale price of said items.

The auction gets off to a slow start. An official National League baseball, signed by several members of the

1998 Cardinals, sells for $50, less than half the estimated sale price of $125. Worse, there is something merciful about the single bid, as if the buyer feels sorry for the auctioneer that there is no other interest in the item. Many subsequent items are withdrawn, after failing to meet their reserves, or to generate any bids at all. Few meet or exceed their estimates. At times, the auctioneer sounds like he's begging.

Ozersky, hands in pockets, shuffles his feet nervously at the back of the room. If this is what an auction is like, he's not sure he wants any part of it. One thing he knows is that when he sells his ball, there won't be any house-coats in his auction. The kind of sale he'd feel most comfortable with would just be a few items, maybe just these eight home run balls, and that's it. Anything more, and he worries his ball might lose the spotlight. However it happens, he decides, it can't happen like this. He looks over at the young woman who caught McGwire's first home run ball, a college student named Kaley Bernsen, and wonders how it is she's not biting her nails and pulling her hair out. He knows that if he hopes to see out-of-control money for his ball—Mike Barnes has told him the serious collectors call what he's looking for "stupid money"—he will have to consider a live sale, but he's not crazy about the idea.

With Barnes priced out of the running, the only two bidders on the McGwire ball, lot #1056, are elsewhere. Two Selkirk representatives with phones to their ears take turns topping each other on behalf of their absentee clients, like some humorless clones of Alphonse and Gaston.

After you, sir.

No, no, no, after you.

Finally, the bidding loses steam at $17,000, and Barnes turns to Ozersky and says, "I guess that means my guy got it." He doesn't reveal who his guy might be, and Ozersky doesn't press him on it.

Kaley Bernsen's mother, Maureen Frank, approaches Ozersky and asks if he would mind posing for a picture with her daughter. "The first and the last," she says.

Ozersky obliges. He even puts his arm around Bernsen, for posterity.

Other photographers snap to the same shot, on the back of the mother's trouble. From the smile on Bernsen's face, it seems she has no idea there had been a bidder—McFarlane—prepared to go as high as $50,000 for her ball. She is genuinely pleased with her take, and figures it'll help pay for a couple years of college, and anyway it's more than she had went she went out to the game. It is a sentiment Ozersky will hear a thousand times before it is all over—from Barnes's other clients, from family and friends, from the place in the back of his mind where the things he doesn't like to think about go to die . . . *Whatever you wind up with, it's more than you had.*

Abbott looks on at all the attention being showered on Ozersky and smiles gamely. A reporter asks what her connection is, to these ball-catching people, and she remarks with good cheer that she is the girlfriend of the ball. It's a line she borrows from her father, and she mentions this as well. He's taken to calling himself the father of the girlfriend of the ball, she says.

On the way out, Barnes lets Ozersky in on his thinking. "I guess this means we take it to New York," he says. The two of them had discussed holding the auction here in St. Louis, possibly through Phillips-Selkirk, in hopes of making the event accessible to as many passionate Cardinals fans as possible. "There was no money in that room," he adds, articulating the obvious. "Both bidders were absentee."

Ozersky concurs, although he doesn't let on the lengths of his concern. All along, he's been thinking he had the stomach for an auction, but now he's not so sure. How do you guarantee you'll have at least two buyers, bidding each other up? Who's to say you won't have just one person trying to buy the ball? What happens then? What happens if there's wild disinterest? Lately he's been thinking $1 million, free and clear, won't be enough to do some of the things he's been thinking about. He wants to open a sports camp for abused children, with his sister Sharon. He wants to make a sizeable donation to the Leukemia Society of America, in memory of Mike Miller, the brother-in-law of Nancy Miller, his former boss down at the lab who arranged for the tickets to the last game of the season. He wants to give money to the American Cancer Society, in memory of his cousin, Bob Goodman. He wants to keep giving to Cardinals Care, in honor of McGwire. He wants to buy a new house for his parents, or pay off their mortgage, or set them up for their retirement. He wants to do a whole lot, he's realizing, and $1 million just won't cut it. It's possible $2 million won't be enough, and he can't imagine anyone going any higher. Even stupid money is not that stupid.

Seven

Greater Fools and Other Theories

Or, For a Few Dollars More

Krathen, Freedland, and Barnes gave themselves a drop-dead date of Thanksgiving weekend to determine their next move. Either Ozersky would sign an agreement to take the ball to auction, or they would conclude a sale with one of Barnes's private bidders.

Ozersky wasn't sure he understood the rush to a decision, but his advisers didn't want this thing stretching out any longer than it already had. There might never be a better time for their client to make a deal. Fan, corporate, and media interest had been spiraling upward since the end of the 1998 baseball season. The auction market was brimming with unique items that promised to lift the sale of the 70th home run ball, and collectors had never been quicker to outspend each other—and, resultingly, to second-guess each other after each sale. The Phillips-Selkirk sale of Mark McGwire's 1st 1998 home run ball was a disappointment, at $17,000 (or, $19,550, with the buyer's surcharge), but Barnes didn't think it offered an accurate read on the market, considering that the winning bidder had been prepared to pay $50,000. Already, Charlie Sheen's $93,500 "Mookie" ball had been dusted by the $126,500 paid by an anonymous buyer for a ball hit in 1923 by Babe Ruth for the first home run hit in Yankee Stadium, despite the fact that many in the hobby doubted the ball's authenticity.

There was such a scramble for these record-setting items that there were at least two public custody battles over the rightful ownership of certain 1998 game balls, one involving a Mark McGwire blast that didn't quite make it over the fence. In the first, a Cubs fan named Gary Mullins contended he was on Waveland Avenue outside Wrigley Field with Sammy Sosa's 62nd home run ball in his hands on September 13, before it was stripped from him in a pileup. Brendan Cunningham, the Chicago mortgage broker who wound up with the ball, was ordered by a judge to keep the ball in a safe deposit box until its ownership could be determined. Mullins eventually dropped his claim, and Cunningham traded the ball back to Sosa for some signed items.

The second battle was played out on national television. Producers for the syndicated courtroom program *The People's Court*, starring former New York City Mayor Edward I. Koch, contacted two disputants over the custody of McGwire's disallowed September 20 home run in

Milwaukee County Stadium and asked them to settle the matter on the show. The ball appeared to have cleared the fence, just beyond the 392-foot sign in left center field, but umpire Bob Davidson maintained that a fan had touched the ball before it left the field and sent McGwire back to second base with a double. Michael Chapes, who was escorted from the stadium and fined $518 for interfering with a ball in play, argued he was in possession of the ball when it cleared the fence but that it was wrested from his glove by a sixteen-year-old named Johnny Luna. Luna was attending the game with the father of one of his friends. The father, Jerry DiGilio, a widowed bridge painter from New York, thought it would be a hoot to take his two sons and two of their friends to see McGwire and Sosa play out their momentous strings, and hopefully snag one of those prized home run balls.

Judge Koch made a careful study of a videotape the program's announcer called "the most scrutinized video since the Zapruder tape," ignoring for the moment that video tape was not widely available in 1963, and ruled in favor of DiGilio and his charge. The former mayor said he applied the rules of the game to his decision; Chapes was evidently not in secure possession of the ball at the time it bounded from his glove and into Luna's hands. The two parties were given generous appearance fees, but the 65½ ball, as it had came to be known, was awarded to Luna, who promptly consigned it to Mastro Fine Sports Auctions for its fall catalogue sale, during which it sold for $22,370, including the surcharge, known in the trade as the buyer's premium.

There was even an aborted sale of Mickey Mantle's so-called "blue balls," inscribed by the Yankee legend with messages like "Fuck You!" and "Willie Mays Sucks," offered by a Las Vegas auction house named Gallery of History. That the balls didn't meet their minimum reserves was taken as a sign that collectors were only interested in items of wholesome and historical value.

Certainly, in such a heated marketplace, Ozersky's ball would command the best possible price, but there were other arguments pointing to a quick sale; most significantly, there was a potential tax bill for 1998, even if the ball didn't sell until 1999. According to Freedland's tax experts, which included George Mundstock, of the University of Miami School of Law, his client would owe money based on the market value of the baseball at the time he received it. The taxable acts, the argument went, were in catching the ball *and* in selling the ball. The gray area was in putting a price on the ball at the moment of acquisition. If Freedland took the published $1 million Ryan-Goodman-Lewis offer as the fair market value on September 27, and adjusted it to reflect a ten-year payout, he could establish a value on the ball at between $200,000 and $350,000 at the time it was caught. (The wide range was owing to the fact that the money was not guaranteed.) Or, he could consider the retail price of an official National League baseball—$10 or so. What stymied Freedland and his tax experts was the fact that the one offer on the table when the ball was hit was only made for the final, record-setting home run. Someone could have reasonably taken the position that as of the seventh inning on the last scheduled date of the season, there was no conclusive way to know whether or not Ozersky's ball would stand as the record.

It was all a matter of interpretation, and Freedland fell on the conservative side. He was inclined to advise Ozersky to pay 1998 taxes, mindful of the fact that his cousin didn't have much in the way of 1998 dollars with which to pay them, which meant he needed a quick sale in order to meet his April 15, 1999 obligation. Freedland calculated that the 1998 federal tax obligation on a ball valued at $250,000, would be $97,500, assuming a 39.6 percent tax bracket.

Freedland didn't like with the way the Internal Revenue Service effectively encouraged the record ball holders to donate their prizes to a not-for-profit institution like the Hall of Fame, referring to comments made during the season by IRS spokespersons. "We'd have to take a look at all the circumstances," the IRS's Steven J. Pyrek told *The New York Times*, responding to questions about how a record baseball might be treated by his agency. Freedland thought it set a dangerous precedent for a government agency to be manipulating private sector activity, even if it was just a subtle form of manipulation. To him, the implication was clear: a twelve-year-old fan could be treated differently from a twenty-six-year-old research scientist, who in turn could be treated differently from a fifty-six-year-old investment banker. Major league baseballs are hit into the stands all the time, and no one had ever been expected to pay any taxes on the receipt of those balls, until now.

Other tax experts didn't necessarily agree with Freedland's. One, Dr. Sheldon D. Pollack, a practicing tax attorney and professor of business law at the University of Delaware, might have advised his client differently on the matter of a 1998 tax burden. "It's a long-standing doctrine," he said, "that if the property doesn't have 'readily ascertained value,' you don't have to take it into taxes until the value becomes fixed and determinable." Ozersky could claim the ball didn't have an established value until

1999, when he would sell it, and the IRS could contest the point, but Pollack felt strongly that Ozersky would prevail.

Noted tax researcher Jim Jenkins, author of the book *Failure to File,* concurred. "The taxable act was not catching the ball," he said, "but selling it."

Another uncertainty over McGwire's 70th home run ball was whether it would be taxed as a capital asset or an ordinary investment. One position was that if Ozersky held the ball for at least one year, it would be taxed as a long-term capital asset, subject to a 28 percent tax, the maximum capital-gains rate on collectibles. If, however, Ozersky was a dealer or trader in sports memorabilia and held it for that same one-year period, he might receive a ruling allowing only a 20 percent tax, the maximum rate for ordinary long-term capital gains. This last scenario would represent a savings of about $200,000 for every $1 million in the sale price of the ball, over the maximum short-term rate of 39.6 percent.

What all of this meant, to Ozersky, was that he should probably sell the ball sooner rather than later to capitalize on the hype of the record-setting season, and the frenzy in the sports collectibles market, and later rather than sooner to capitalize on more favorable long-term tax rates.

It was enough to make a person's head explode. Or spin. Or do something other than think clearly.

Perhaps the most obvious argument for selling the ball before the start of the 1999 season was that records—even home run records that eclipsed by more than 16 percent the record that had stood for the previous thirty-six seasons—were made to be broken. Few people in baseball thought it likely that McGwire, or anyone else, would hit 70 home runs in consecutive seasons, but fewer still had thought it could be done the first time. Ozersky was not about to gamble on this one—not with his future on the line, and the charitable causes he had lately taken up as his own—and Krathen, Freedland, and Barnes were not about to advise him to do so.

The shared thinking, therefore, was to maximize Ozersky's return on the ball, and sell before the bottom dropped on what appeared to be a burgeoning marketplace. The tax considerations were key, but there would be time to figure them out later. The thing to do, Ozersky's three wise men began to realize, was sell. And soon.

"Selling art has much in common with selling root beer," observed one-time Sotheby's head Adolph Alfred Taubman to a *Wall Street Journal* reporter. "People don't need root beer and they don't need to buy a painting either. We provide them with a sense that it will give them a happier existence."

Such was the sense that Ozersky and company were getting as they leaned toward auction. The McFarlane and Bamm Beano deals were still percolating out of Mike Barnes's cramped St. Louis offices, and there were several intriguing new offers to consider, but the consensus was that an auction held the richest possible return. It also held the highest risk, although Freedland and Barnes had been working to minimize those risks. What they were hearing, from the various auction houses looking for Ozersky's consignment, was that the highest minimum reserve ever placed on a baseball was $50,000, but they had been able to negotiate that number to $500,000 at several auction houses. The higher the minimum reserve, they maintained, the greater Ozersky's comfort level; if the ball didn't reach his price, he could always withdraw it and pursue a private sale, or hold the ball until the market improved.

One house, Guernsey's, was even willing to consider a minimum reserve of $1.25 million, reflecting the written offers already in hand. Arlan Ettinger, a smallish, soft-spoken man whose friends called him Rusty, even though the hair that might have justified the name was now either gone or gray, swallowed hard before agreeing to this last, because as Ozersky's comfort level increased his went down like an anvil. He could devote all kinds of money and energy to a successful sale and still see the ball withdrawn at what would have once been thought an astronomical price. But he took Barnes and Freedland at their word and figured that if that kind of money was there in a private sale, it would be there at auction. Ettinger mentioned the figure to colleagues, and they thought he was nuts to establish a reserve ten times greater than the previous record sale for a similar item, but he was going with his instinct. He wanted the ball, and if this was what it took to win the consignment, then this was what it took.

The other auction houses were all willing to negotiate, but Krathen and Freedland wanted to do business with Guernsey's, and as each day passed it took a bit more for Ettinger to close the deal. Soon, it took a small slice of Guernsey's catalogue sales—$5 per—after Ettinger reported to Barnes that he sold more than 100,000 catalogues at his JFK auction and that this time around he would arrange with Amazon.com or Barnes & Noble to make the book available over the Internet. It took a promise to spend at least $250,000 to promote and stage the sale. And it took negotiating away his seller's commission—first to 10 percent from the customary 15, then to 8, then to 5, then to 3. Ettinger would still make his money on the buyer's premium (15 percent on the first $1 million, 12 percent on the next $1 million, and 5 percent thereafter), and the McGwire ball was exactly the sort of marquee item around which he could built an entire sale. Plus, if circumstances fell to his advantage, he could count on Barnes's other clients to follow Ozersky into the deal, and then Guernsey's would be in a position to build something special. The theme of the auction could be "The Great Home Run Balls in Baseball History." There was no telling what other items might turn up.

The appeal of an auction, to an edge-seeking guy like Barnes, was the way it could shake money from the buyers' tree. In a private sale, a bidder would never know if he was negotiating against himself, because as the stakes reached higher the bidder would worry he was overpaying for an item no one else wanted. Barnes knew about the psychology of auctions. He knew about buyer's remorse and stupid money and adrenaline spending. He knew about the importance of the order of sale. He knew about the greater fool theory, which held that no matter how high the price at a heated auction, the previous bidder was always in as nearly as deep as the winning bidder. The winning bidder may in fact prove to have been a fool, but at least he will have had company.

The drawback was that, after establishing a comfortable minimum reserve, the auction was completely out of your client's control. It had been important to Ozersky to direct the ball into what he felt were the right set of hands. Yes, he wanted it to net the highest possible return, but he also wanted it to be put on display. He wanted to ensure that it wasn't shredded, or locked away in some bank vault, or openly exploited in some unanticipated way. He wanted to know that whoever bought it would be a good caretaker of McGwire's legacy, as he hoped to have been. On some days, he even wanted to remain connected to the ball, as kind of a spokesperson. He wanted a lot, actually, for a guy who was so eager to sell, but Barnes was determined to see that he got it.

It was what he did, now, for a living.

Among the intriguing new offers for Ozersky to consider were a revised push from the guy who had made a market in the Berlin Wall and Dallas Cowboys turf and a tax-advantaged lease arrangement proposed by a Florida businessman, who happened to be Michael Freedland's father-in-law.

Gary Summers wasn't sure what he would ultimately do with the ball. He just had to have it. It was, to him, baseball's Holy Grail, and he pursued it like a mercenary combination of King Arthur and John Cleese. He developed optic concept prototypes for premium giveaway items, which he hoped to market through McDonald's or Wheaties. He explored using hologram imagery of the ball on a special-issue MasterCard offering. And then he hit on what might have been the mother of all marketing plans—a thing he liked to call "Fantasy Home Run Game #70."

Okay, so maybe the title needed some work, but Summers felt sure the concept was sound: a computer reenactment of the 70th home run, with the chance for over one million fans to "catch" the ball all over again. Summers would team with one of the big broadcast or cable outlets—Turner, Fox Sports, ESPN—and secure the participation of Mark McGwire, through his representative Jim Milner. Then he'd market tickets corresponding to actual seat locations in all thirty major league baseball stadiums, at $100 each. There would have to be a simple trivia question component to the promotion, to remove it from gambling or lottery status and allow fan participation in all fifty states, but Summers didn't see that as any kind of problem. What he saw, mostly, was money. Lots of it. He projected ticket sales would generate $126 million, and there would be room in his on-air simulation for commercials and other revenue-generating opportunities.

Ozersky could sell Summers the ball outright—Summers told Barnes his investors were willing to pay as much as $5 million for the ball, with some expression of interest from McGwire—or he could cut himself a piece of the deal. It was up to him. At $126 million, there'd be plenty to go around, even after that hot shot Ford salesman took his share.

The other offer was more feet-on-the-ground than pie-in-the-sky, but it was encumbered by a potential conflict of interest and some uncertain answers to pending tax questions. Edd Helms, a Florida businessman who at one point devoted his primary energies to placing facsimile machines in hotels nationwide, couldn't help it that his daughter Charlene had married Michael Freedland. They'd been married a year, and the kid still called him Mr. Helms, but the relationship didn't have to cost Helms a deal. Freedland agreed. He instructed Barnes to handle all negotiations with Mr. Helms, and to consult directly with Ozersky.

Helms recognized the tax implications on the receipt and sale of the ball, and the push to sell it quickly, and he built his proposal accordingly. He offered to purchase exclusive rights to the ball for $2 million, plus a royalty of nine percent on net profits from memorabilia and souvenir sales, advertising rights, exhibitions and income-producing activities of any kind, including the eventual resale of the ball itself. Payment was to be structured in a lease arrangement, in consideration of Ozersky's tax burden: a $75,000 deposit on signing; a second $75,000 payment by January 15, 1999; $100,000 by March 1, 1999; and the remaining $1,750,000 to be paid by October 31, 1999. In addition, Helms offered to pay Ozersky a rental fee of $25,000 per month for marketing rights to the ball until the sale was concluded.

The main appeal of the Helms deal was the chance to save 19.6 percent in federal taxes (or, $196,000, for every $1 million in the sale price), assuming the IRS would allow Ozersky to file under the 20 percent capital gain rate on investments held for more than one year. This was a large assumption, but failing such a favorable ruling, he would at least save 11.6 percent in filing under the long-term capital asset rate of 28 percent (or, $116,000 per $1 million). Either way, it was hard to argue with the numbers: Ozersky would have to sell the ball for $2.65 million in an immediate, private sale to realize the same after-tax windfall as he would in the $2 million, long-term capital gain scenario. More, he stood to earn an additional percentage on ongoing merchandising efforts and on the eventual re-sale of the ball, driving the value of the deal even higher.

Helms couldn't see this Ozersky kid doing any better.

There were times, during these extensive deliberations and contemplations, when Mike Barnes felt like he, Krathen, Freedland, and Ozersky were among the College of Cardinals, holed up in the Vatican, and the auctioneers and memorabilia dealers were waiting impatiently outside for the first puff of smoke to filter forth from the chimney. A siege mentality set in, and the rest of the world fell away until his colleagues and their client could come to a decision.

They got closer, by degrees. They agreed to agree in principle with Guernsey's to conduct a live sale at Madison Square Garden at the earliest possible date—perhaps in late December, before the Christmas holiday, or in early January. It was a commitment with an out clause, allowing the Ozersky camp to continue to negotiate a private sale while Guernsey's moved forward in its plans to stage an auction. Ozersky pledged not to consign the ball to any other auction house and to compensate Ettinger for any out-of-pocket preliminary costs if he should sell the ball before formally placing it with Guernsey's. In addition to the piece of the catalogue sales and the reduced seller's commission, Barnes was also able to negotiate for Ozersky a right of refusal on any additional items to be included in the auction. More and more, Ozersky worried that his ball might be overshadowed by too many other items. He wanted the focus to be on his ball. He didn't mind that Barnes's other clients would join him in the auction, but he wanted to limit it to the record home run balls. He didn't want any surprises.

While Ettinger prepared the contracts, Barnes used the extra few days to continue discussions with his private buyers. Todd McFarlane's last and best offer included the chance for Ozersky to retain partial ownership of the ball, and to participate in any profits or resale, but the up-front money topped out at $1.75 million, and Ozersky wasn't sure he wanted the ball to run his life any more than it already had. Barnes's other clients were split on whether they could improve at auction over what McFarlane was offering, but McFarlane wasn't interested in the entire lineup without Ozersky's ball to anchor his marketing efforts. Absent the 70 ball, he would only be a buyer of one of the record balls, and to his thinking, the coolest of the "lesser" balls was Kerry Woodson's, McGwire's 69th and penultimate home run of the season. Woodson, for his part, wasn't keen on taking his chances in an auction, and he agreed to sell his ball to McFarlane for $200,000, plus unspecified "fringe benefits." The terms of the deal, and the buyer, would not be revealed until February 1999.

The Salvino's Bamm Beano proposal was somewhat richer than it was on first pass, but the distributor would not increase the guaranteed monies to Ozersky and Albert Chapa, the holder of Sammy Sosa's 66th home run ball. They would, however, commit in writing to shipping three to five million McGwire and Sosa bears, which at 50 cents per for Ozersky meant an additional $1.5 million on top of the $1 million advance payment. This was a lot, even Barnes would admit, but he worried his client would only see the back-end money in a successful sell-through; if Salvino's was left holding too many bean bags, Ozersky and Chapa would have a hard time collecting any payments due.

Freedland used the down time to complete a background check on the auction house. He had hired a private investigator named Garnett Samuels to look into Guernsey's business dealings and Ettinger's personal affairs and learned that the company had an excellent credit rating, and far fewer claims from creditors or disgruntled buyers and sellers than comparably sized auction houses. They paid their bills on time—one week sooner than most of their competitors.

Meanwhile, Ozersky's "lesser" suitors continued to

scramble for a deal. Among them, Helms and Summers put finishing touches to their proposals, but there were significant hurdles to each. The Helms deal made sense if Ozersky could be assured of the more favorable tax treatment, but such assurances were not forthcoming. Moreover, there were too many opportunities for the buyer to exit the deal prior to October 31, 1999, when the sale would be completed, and Ozersky did not want to chance another record-setting season with the ball still in his possession.

The Summers deal was handicapped by McGwire's apparent disinterest. Summers's investors were willing to back his fantasy home run concept if the slugger would agree to at least consider some level of participation, but without even a grudging endorsement they could not see investing too heavily. What this meant, for Ozersky, was that his payday on this deal would have to be on the come, and here again he was uneasy about the risks. There were no sure things, he knew, but he figured he would do well to at least eliminate as many of the uncertainties as possible.

Eight

A Somewhat Better Day in the Life of a Research Scientist

December 8, 1998

Philip Ozersky hasn't spent this much time with his prized baseball since . . . well, he guesses he's never spent this much time with it. He caught it on a Sunday, slept with it beside his bed that first night, put it in his girlfriend's parents' safe on Monday, placed it in a

NationsBank safe deposit box on Tuesday, and parked it at the Cardinals Hall of Fame the following week.

Even when he's gone to visit the ball—to show it to his friends, to have his picture taken with it—it's like it's been in intensive care. From the moment it was first put on display, it has been monitored by 24-hour security, and insured by the Fireman's Fund for $1.5 million, at a premium to Ozersky of $1,330. Whenever it's gone from one venue to the next, or accompanied Ozersky to a media interview, it has been moved with its own entourage: off-duty police, uniformed police, and, once, a private security guard. It was an increasing frustration, the way the ball had so many protective layers around it. Ozersky couldn't touch the thing without at least one set of well-trained eyes on him, and if you'd have put it to him in just these terms he would have understood how Woody Allen must have felt, visiting his kid under restraining order.

And yet here, in New York, the city with one of the highest crime rates in the world, the one place (other than a too-small and too-heavily-shrubbed backyard) where a baseball is most likely to be lost, it is being transported by backpack. Ozersky's got the thing wrapped in a baggie and zippered into his black and blue ACG-Karst 25 model, sharing a main pocket with a bottle of springwater pinched from his hotel room. When someone points out that perhaps it's not such a good idea to keep a bottle of water so perilously close to his ball—what if it spills?—he shrugs his shoulders and says, "Oh."

Ozersky's in town for a press conference to announce the ball's consignment to Guernsey's, a Manhattan auction house specializing in one-of-a-kind sales, and to surrender the ball to Guernsey's president Arlan Ettinger, and he's not about to entrust such a special delivery to anyone else. Plus, this'll likely be the last chance he gets to handle the ball on his own terms. Legally, the ball will remain his until the auction, which is scheduled for January 12, at 7 P.M., at Madison Square Garden, but for all practical purposes, this is it.

Ozersky waffled about as long as he could. At the next-to-the-last moment, before deciding conclusively to take the ball to auction, the Edd Helms lease proposal started to look pretty good. Barnes and Helms were able to resolve every open issue, and for a while it seemed there'd be a deal. Helms even trademarked the phrase "70th Home Run Ball," and secured the same Internet domain name, thinking the deal was moving forward. He began designing a line of clothing, carrying the "70th Home Run Ball" phrase and logo. He was nearly in business. Barnes and Freedland had to notify Guernsey's that Ozersky was pulling his ball from the auction, and Ettinger was furious. Without the 70th home run ball, he had no sale, and here he was readying a major press conference and lining up other items to bring to Ozersky for his approval.

And then, just as the next-to-the-last moment gave way to the last, the wind blew Ozersky's thinking back in its previous direction. There was just too much to think about. He didn't get why he had to make a move so quickly. He understood that the Law Offices of David Krathen had other business to conduct, and paying clients to serve, and he knew it was a good time to move on a sale, but he had never been any good at making these kinds of decisions. What looked good one moment seemed suspect the next.

Before Ettinger learned of Ozersky's turnaround back

to auction, Freedland used the moment to his client's advantage. He pressed Ettinger into cutting Ozersky's seller's commission down to zero. Ozersky's indecision wasn't meant as a negotiating ploy, but it was certainly an opening, and Freedland felt he would be doing his client a disservice in letting it close. Ettinger felt he had no choice but to accept these new terms. It was somewhat onerous, to face the prospect of working so hard to achieve the highest possible sale price on an item with no payment due him from the seller, but he'd invested too much of his time and his company's money to lose the ball. And besides, there would still be the buyer's premium added to the winning bid.

It was perhaps the first time in Arlan Ettinger's auction career that zero seemed better than nothing.

There's a sad baseball backdrop to today's announcement: Yankee great Joe DiMaggio, who's been in Memorial Regional Hospital in Hollywood, Florida since October battling what was at first reported to be pneumonia, has apparently taken a turn for the worse, and from the media maneuverings in evidence among the reporters gathering to cover the Guernsey's press conference, a kind of deathwatch has set in. There's an urgent message on the wires suggesting that the man who is perhaps more closely associated with the great Yankees teams of the past than anyone else might not make it through another night.

At eighty-three, Joe DiMaggio's stature as the preeminent sports hero in a sports-minded town is such that New York news editors cannot be caught short in the event of his death. His obituary, as it is with most larger-than-life personages of advancing age, has already been

written and set in type at the major metropolitan newspapers, and appropriate "B-roll" footage has been com-
piled by local broadcast outlets. And yet, underneath the
cruel realities of the news business, there emerges an
even more heartless truth: DiMaggio's demise, if it comes
to pass, threatens to take with it the hoped-for coverage
of Guernsey's home run ball auction.

One story kills the other.

Unaware of the drama unfolding in DiMaggio's Florida
hospital room (or the effect it might have on his own
adventure), Ozersky hops a cab with Amanda Abbott
from the Marriott Marquis Hotel to Trump Tower, where
the press conference is to be held. They ride with Mike
Barnes, the agent the *New York Post* says "has run down
more balls than Willie Mays," and John Grass, the school
district groundskeeper who absorbed the lightning rod's
share of criticism for deciding to keep McGwire's 63rd
home run ball. As they squeeze into the yellow medallion
cab, they are welcomed by a prerecorded message from
talk show host Sally Jesse Raphael, telling them to buckle
up. The greeting is part of a city-wide taxi campaign, in-
corporating the voices of well-known New Yorkers (including Judd Hirsch, of TV's *Taxi!*), and there's another
message for when they leave. This one seems too pre-
scient to have been prerecorded: Ozersky has got his pre-
cious cargo, and Grass had got his ball secured in a fanny
pack, and as they stretch out of the cab they hear Sally
Jesse again, telling them to take their valuables with
them. As if they need reminding.

Beyond the DiMaggio bulletin, the most immediate
crisis of the morning greets Barnes on his way through
the gilded front doors of Trump Tower. Heath Wiseman,
the vet student who snared McGwire's 68th, was supposed

to have sent his ball from Iowa to New York via Federal Express, but Guernsey's Ettinger informs him in the lobby that the ball has been rerouted to California. All the other balls have arrived—Vern Kuhlemeier's 64th Sosa ball, Albert Chapa's 66th Sosa ball, Doug Singer's 67th McGwire ball—and have been placed in display cases in the Trump Tower lobby for the press conference. (Jason King decided to keep his 64th McGwire ball out of the auction, believing he could do better in a private sale at a later date.) Ettinger's also got Sosa's 61st home run ball, which has been donated to the auction by the Chicago Cubs, with 97 percent of the proceeds to benefit the Hurricane Georges relief effort in the Dominican Republic. Sosa himself is even scheduled to attend the press conference, to promote the sale of the 61st home run ball and the various good works of the Sammy Sosa Charitable Foundation. What's missing, Ettinger reports, is Wiseman's ball, and the auctioneer is not happy about it. True, a display case featuring six of these record balls will not be measurably less effective as a selling tool than a display case featuring seven, but Ettinger's been after Barnes's clients to get their items to him for several days. He doesn't get why something this important must be left until the last minute.

"California?" Barnes says. This is news to him, but when he is assured that the ball has been tracked, and located, and reshipped to Guernsey's for next day delivery, he lets it slide. He's got about a million things to worry about, so he moves on to the other 999,999.

One of the front-and-center worries, for Ozersky, is the confirmation that Sosa will soon arrive. This had been discussed, in theory, but he never quite believed the slugger would show, and now it appears Ozersky's unprepared. He needs a baseball for Sosa to sign, and a Sharpie pen for him to sign it with, because there's no way Ozersky is going to share the stage with a hero like Sammy Sosa without getting his autograph. He's sorry, but there's just no way.

Ozersky moves into action, same way he did back in that party box at Busch, more than two months earlier. He gets his mind around a thing, and he goes for it. He pulls Ettinger from an important-seeming conversation with one of his public relations people and asks for the location of the nearest sporting goods store. He runs the two long city blocks to a Modell's on Fifty-Seventh Street and purchases the last four official Rawlings National League balls from a rack by the counter. Then he stops at Staples for some black Sharpies and races back to Trump Tower, where Sosa's limousine is idling out front, on Fifth Avenue. The Cubs right fielder has arrived about a half hour ahead of schedule, and his handlers decide to have him circle the block a couple times rather than have him mill about the Trump Tower lobby with nothing to do.

Donald Trump, meanwhile, is ensconced upstairs in his corporate offices, waiting for the signal from *his* handlers that Sosa has arrived. Clearly, these two men are the dog and pony of Guernsey's show, and it's apparent neither wants to be seen waiting for the other, although it seems not to matter that fifty or sixty members of the press have gathered in the lobby and are themselves waiting.

Ozersky, waiting, is coaxed through a half-dozen, same-seeming interviews by Guernsey's press representative, Ron Berkowitz of the Manhattan-based public relations firm Rubenstein Associates. By now, Ozersky can usually respond to these questions without thinking, although occasionally he'll be left scratching his head at the carelessness on the part of some of the reporters. There's one guy, from *The New York Daily News,* who seems to gather his thoughts in one area before pulling questions from someplace else. "So," this enterprising reporter probes, "this must be, like, an early Christmas present for you, in a way."

It's not clear if this is a question, but Ozersky assumes that it is. "Actually, no," he says. "The auction is in January. It's right there on the press release. It's more like a late-Christmas present."

"Right," the reporter says, fumbling for his copy of the press release, as if he knew this all along. "When I said early, I meant early in terms of, you know, summer, and now."

Another reporter wants to understand if Ozersky prefers to be known as a ball owner or a ball catcher. "What's the correct term?" the reporter asks, as if this is something Ozersky might have filled in on some form, somewhere.

About the only concern for Ozersky in this latest round of questions are the requests to reflect on the life and career of Joe DiMaggio. At first, he is not entirely clear why these reporters are soliciting note and comment from the likes of him, a simple geneticist who happened to catch a baseball of significant public interest. If it was Stan Musial they were talking about, then maybe he could see how his thoughts could be made relevant, him being a Cardinals fan and all. But Joe DiMaggio? He knows where he fits in the pantheon, he knows that to New Yorkers he's right up there with Ruth and Gehrig and Mantle, but he never saw him play. His father was a big Brownies fan, so he must have seen DiMaggio play when the Yankees came to St. Louis, but he never talked about him much. So, really, what can Ozersky add to the man's record?

"He was a great ballplayer," he tries at one point, when pressed for at least some kind of response. "I wish him well."

Sosa finally tires of circling. He is led into the building through a back entrance and brought upstairs for a face-to-face with Trump, during which time the two apparently trade fashion secrets; when they come down to the lobby they match—sort of. Sosa's got on a yellow-tinted pair of happening sunglasses while Trump sports a yellow-tinted mop of happened hair. On both heads, the shade is striking for the way it has absolutely nothing to do with any color found in nature; it suggests a look that gets along far better with the baseball player than it does with the tycoon.

Ettinger steps to the microphone and makes his announcement. He calls the upcoming sale "one of the most exciting auctions of the decade," and "one of the most sought-after collections in the history of auctions." He speaks in exclamation points, especially when introducing a representative from eBay, the on-line auction house and darling of Wall Street speculators, which has teamed with Guernsey's to handle the sale on the Internet. He gives the microphone to eBay's press representative Kristin Sewell, who reports that the auction site currently features more than six thousand Mark McGwire and Sammy Sosa items. A dozen reporters dutifully jot the number down in their notebooks

Then Ettinger introduces Sosa and Trump, and the deathwatch kicks in:

"Sammy, a message for Joe D.?"

"Mr. Trump, you've met DiMaggio. Any recollections?"

"¿Qué piensas de la carera de Joe DiMaggio? ¿De su reputación?"

Trump, to his credit, does an expert job deflecting attention back to Sosa and the Guernsey's auction, with no disrespect to the Yankee legend. He answers the first few questions politely, and finds ways to connect the values and work ethic of DiMaggio with those same qualities in athletes like Sammy Sosa and Mark McGwire. Sosa, for his part, struggles through the language barrier to keep the focus on the 1998 season, on the home run balls, on the efforts of his foundation to fly in food and clothing to the people of his homeland. He is appropriately deferential in speaking about DiMaggio, but he returns the talk to the auction at first chance, and to the devastation of his people.

Still, the reporters do not let up, determined as they are to land their sound bite on what more and more appears to be the likely death of the Yankee legend. After a while of this, each successive query brings a low groaning from those in the crowd with a vested interest in the auction: the Guernsey's and Rubenstein people, the eBay people, the ball owners (or is it ball catchers?), the Trump Tower staff.

Ettinger, himself one of the low groaners, seems to want to cut the questioning short. Ozersky sits nervously in the front row. He's not sure he likes the way the press conference is going, but he does not appear as troubled by it as Ettinger and his public relations team. Perhaps he doesn't know enough about the media-hyping business to be troubled by it. Perhaps it's because the DiMaggio situation keeps presenting itself in the form of questions he's not sure how to answer. Most likely, though, it's because it no longer seems likely Ozersky will get a chance to visit with Sosa, or have him sign his baseballs. In truth, he'll say later, this last takes up more space in his thinking than he'd like to admit. His head is filled with what he might say to Sosa. Maybe he'll ask him a question about Roberto Clemente, see if he can get the man to connect his career and his efforts off the field to the Hall of Famer. Also, he's wondering if he should bother asking Donald Trump for his autograph as well. He's calculating what it might be worth to get the two of them, Sosa and Trump, to put their signatures on the same baseball.

Back at the lab . . .

Philip Ozersky's colleagues at the Genome Sequencing Center are preparing for a press conference of a different kind. On Friday, the journal *Science* is slated to announce the successful mapping of a worm genome, the result of a years-long project headed jointly by Robert H. Waterston of Washington University, in St. Louis, and John E. Sulston of the Sanger Center, located outside Cambridge, England.

The sequencing breakthrough is arguably one of the most significant biological developments in recent years, although it is one that many scientists had seen coming. Biologists have long found worms and humans to have many genes in common, and following the sequencing of the worm DNA the mapping of the human genome is thought to be inevitable. Prior to this study, scientists have only been able to map single-cell organisms like bacteria.

Ozersky's end of the years-long study has been mostly logged in front of the computer, closing the gaps in the technologically regenerated worm sequence. It's like looking at a map of the world, he says, and focusing in on smaller and smaller areas of detail. In the production lab, his colleagues worked tirelessly to sequence random pieces of DNA in order to create a map of the whole, and sometimes the space between one segment and the next needed to be filled in after a more directed analysis of available data.

The genome of the worm in question, a microscopic roundworm that goes by the scientific name of Caenorhabditis elegans, was discovered to contain 19,099 genes and 97 million chemical units. According to Ozersky, the corresponding DNA sequence, reduced to his component parts and laid end to end, would stretch from the Gateway Arch monument in St. Louis to San Francisco's Golden Gate Bridge—from the symbol of McGwire's new town to the symbol of his old. When completed, the human genome sequence will likely stretch from the Earth to the Moon, and back.

The breakthrough carries profound implications in the study and treatment of genetic-based diseases, and for the manager of the center's finishing lab, it is a fairly heady feeling, to be out on the cutting edges of science and technology.

"It certainly puts this ball in perspective," Ozersky allows.

Nine

Promises, Promises

*Or, How Does
Your Garden Grow?*

The sports auction community didn't know what to make of Arlan Ettinger's pending sale. His competitors couldn't see where Guernsey's would make its money, if all Ettinger could offer were the McGwire and Sosa balls. They couldn't be too critical of his strategy, because they had all been willing to accept pretty much the same terms, but now that they had lost out on the business, the impulse was to second guess.

Ettinger, too, felt he had to grow his auction to cover his bets. He'd finagled himself into a tight spot. He knew he had to consider other items to round out his sale. Some of the items came to him, some he went looking for.

He needed to generate enough money to make up for the seller's commission he had given away, and he felt it was inevitable that the auction expand beyond the original home run balls. He didn't want for consignments. Every private collector in the country had something for him to consider: baseballs, bats, cleats, a full set of architectural blueprints for the original Yankee Stadium. You name it.

Guernsey's hired Richard Simon, a noted autograph and sports memorabilia expert, to sort through the proposals and assemble a collection worthy of a premier item like Ozersky's baseball. Ettinger wanted to keep his pledge to the young man, to keep the attention on the home run race of 1998, to keep the auction small, but he wasn't doing this for his health, and the 70th home run ball was proving a tremendous magnet to consignors and dealers. It was hard to look away from the lure of McGwire's fantastic accomplishment, or from what such an exciting auction might mean to his small company. Ettinger could have built the sale to include a couple hundred items, easy, but that wasn't what it was supposed to be about, and he meant to honor his commitments.

At some undetermined point in early to middle December, Ettinger spoke to Richard Arndt, the former Milwaukee Brewers' groundskeeper, about including Hank Aaron's 755th home run ball in the sale. Ettinger would say later that Arndt reached out to him; Arndt would claim it was Ettinger who initiated contact. Previously, Arndt had been in discussions with Mike Barnes, about possibly representing the ball and bringing it to auction, and Barnes dutifully reported those discussions to Freedland and Ozersky.

More than any other item under consideration, the

Aaron ball promised to give Ozerksy a run for his money; some in the hobby believed that, as collectible and as marketing tool, it might even be more valuable than the McGwire ball. Ozersky's first thought was to use his right of refusal to ensure that the ball would not be included in the Guernsey's auction. He had nothing against Arndt, but there were other ways for him to sell his ball than on the back of his, and he instructed Freedland to reject the item.

Despite the veto, Ozersky woke up on the morning of December 18 and read in *USA Today* that the Aaron ball would be included in the auction, and he was torn between livid and pragmatic. A part of him didn't want to see the ball at *his* auction (in another inevitability, he had started to look on the Guernsey's sale with a proprietary interest), and another part felt he should consider it. He could, by contract, prevent the Aaron ball from being sold at Madison Square Garden on January 12; in fact, he had attempted to do just that. What he couldn't even attempt to do was keep Arndt from selling it elsewhere, or even through Guernsey's on some other date. Barnes and Freedland suggested that if the Aaron ball was going to be on the market, it would have the same effect on the sale price of the McGwire ball no matter if it sold before, during, or after the auction. If it was during the auction, at least Ozersky could maintain some control. He might even be able to profit from it.

Freedland wasn't torn. He was just livid. His client had a contractual agreement with Ettinger, and here he had to read in the newspaper how the man was openly ignoring that agreement. He called Guernsey's to see if perhaps the *USA Today* account was inaccurate. Ettinger wasn't available, but a member of his staff assured Freedland that, yes, the Aaron ball was to be included in the auction.

"No, it's not," Freedland replied.

"I'm afraid it is," the staffer said, unaware of the extent of the misunderstanding.

"Well, then, Philip's ball is out," Freedland said. "Tell Arlan to take his pick."

Next, Freedland contacted Ettinger's attorney, Richard Herzfeld, to express his dissatisfaction. In a follow-up facsimile transmission sent later that morning, he wrote that he was "shocked and dismayed" to have to learn of Guernsey's plans to include the Aaron ball in a national newspaper, and called the development a professional embarrassment. He referred Herzfeld to the consignment agreement, which gave Ozersky the right to approve "any item consigned for auction which is not one of the home run baseballs by Sammy Sosa or Mark McGwire." The clause, Freedland maintained, was central to his client's decision to take his ball to auction, where it was to be the centerpiece of attention. "This is certainly no longer the case," Freedland wrote.

Ettinger called back promptly, as Freedland knew he would, and at the other end of the call, he and Freedland agreed to share Guernsey's fee on the sale of the Aaron ball—a 5 percent seller's commission and a 15 percent buyer's premium—pending Ozersky's approval.

When Barnes heard about the deal, he noted that Arndt should have hired him to handle his negotiations. His other clients were only paying a 3 percent seller's commission, Ozersky wasn't paying anything, and all of them were receiving a portion of the catalogue sales, plus travel expenses to New York to attend the auction. He also thought it was a workable solution, this 50-50 split on the Aaron ball. It gave Ettinger the chance to make back some of the commission money he had negotiated away, without requiring too much in the way of additional effort or expense, and it offered Ozersky a nice bonus for waiving his refusal.

Ozersky was tired of the constant negotiating, the ups and downs. He had thought that when he consigned the ball to Guernsey's, the uncertainty would disappear. He didn't have the energy for it anymore. It had been three months since he caught the ball, and it was like his life had been on hold since. His entire focus had been on the ball. He couldn't concentrate at work. His relationships were all flatlined by his circumstance: his parents, his siblings, his friends, his co-workers . . . all they ever talked about was the ball. What was he going to do with it? Where is it? How's he going to spend all that money? What's changed? Even his relationship with Amanda had been consumed by what the ball represented. It was hanging over every moment, every conversation, every possibility.

And so he thought, *What the hell.* If someone wanted to give him $100,000 to make that tension go away, it was fine with him.

Predictably, the tension didn't go away entirely, or even for very long. Several days later, Guernsey's faxed to Barnes and Freedland a proposed list of 24 additional items to be included in the auction, for their client's approval.

Ozersky's representatives knew their client well enough at this point to predict which items he'd approve and which he'd reject. There was Mark McGwire's 16th home run ball from the 1998 season, at 545 feet the longest home run of his career, and his 44th, which set a Cardinals team record for most home runs in a single season. Given the original theme of the Guernsey's auction, they knew Ozersky would have no problem with items such as these—and it was a good thing, too, because Barnes had referred both consignors to Guernsey's in the first place. But there were other items of indistinct merit. There was a Jim Thorpe autographed baseball, a plaque presented by Babe Ruth to Rogers Hornsby, a Derek Jeter jersey. Barnes and Freedland didn't doubt the authenticity of any of these thrown-in items, or their value to those in the hobby, but they doubted their client would want them included in the auction.

They also knew their client was too nice a guy to reject any of these items personally, should Ettinger corner him directly before they had a chance to brief him about the list. It was possible Ettinger knew the same, or maybe he felt he had to move quickly to meet his January 12 auction date, because that's just what happened. Ettinger personally presented Ozersky with the list and encouraged him to sign off on most of the proposed items.

Freedland took this as another end around and was once again prepared to advise Ozersky to pull his ball from the auction. Freedland thought it was a cheap tactic for Ettinger to negotiate directly with a consignor he knew to have outside representation, and he called Ettinger on it at first chance. There followed, both men would later recall, another in a series of increasingly strained conversations, and at the other end of this one, Ettinger dropped a tiny bombshell. Once again, Freedland made careful notes, not wanting to miss a word. Okay, Ettinger said. Let's set all these other items aside. There's really only one additional item I'd like to include in the auction and if you agree it'll be the last you'll hear from me on any of this.

Freedland was curious. What is it? he asked.

Mickey Mantle's 500th home run ball, Ettinger replied.

Freedland paused to let the bulletin register. His quick study of the collectibles market told him that Mantle items were far more valuable than Aaron items, and that both, up until this season, were far more valuable than McGwire items. He also knew that the Mantle ball would likely see an inflated price at a New York "event" auction, like the one Guernsey's was staging at Madison Square Garden. He didn't know what kind of condition the ball was in, or its provenance, but he thought of it as another million-dollar item. It could sell for more, it could sell for less, but it was up there.

Same deal as on the Aaron ball, he finally said, not really asking.

Ettinger had figured these guys would seek the precedent they'd set on the Aaron ball, and he knew his bargaining position was not what it could be. Same deal, he said.

Ozersky took in this latest proposal with what he could find of a positive attitude. He tried to think of it as another $100,000 in his pocket. He took the prospect of this $100,000 and added it to the prospect of the $100,000 on the Aaron ball, and the prospect of the $300,000 on the Don Marquess photograph deal. He was furious at the hoops through which he was still being made to jump, and he was anxious as hell. But he was also smiling. A half million dollars. Without even selling the ball.

* * *

Eric Moriarty knew what opportunity looked like. As the sports marketing program manager for eBay, the world's leading on-line auction site, Moriarty had been watching for an opening to the high-end sports collectibles market. It didn't take a genius to figure these McGwire and Sosa balls as his company's key.

In early December, Moriarty struck a partnership deal with Guernsey's, allowing eBay to list the home run balls in its internet catalogue, and allowing its customers to make preliminary bids. The shared thinking was that Guernsey's would benefit from the additional exposure of its auction, and eBay would benefit by introducing its service to thousands of collectors who had never thought to make their purchases on-line.

Guernsey's Ettinger knew on-line auctions were the way of the future. He knew Sotheby's was launching its own on-line auction service. He thought that by aligning with eBay he could at least claim some of the credit for bringing the auction world into the electronic age. Anyway, he wasn't too worried. An on-line environment could never replace the excitement of a live auction. And, in real terms, he didn't have anything to lose; any seller's commission or buyer's premium due Guernsey's would not be shared by eBay, even if an item sold to an on-line bidder.

The initial arrangement called for eBay to open its service to bidders beginning January 5, one week before the Guernsey's auction. Only the McGwire and Sosa home run balls would be available. Minimum bids were established of $100,000 for the 70th home run ball and $50,000 for the lesser balls. The high bidder at the end of eBay's preauction event, which was slated to run through January 11, would establish the floor bid for Guernsey's live auction and be allowed to continue bidding on the corresponding item on-line throughout the live auction the following evening.

It wasn't an ideal system, but at least it was a system. As conceived, it seemed unlikely that the high eBay bidders would have any chance of competing with in-person and telephone bidders on the night of the live auction. By late December, there were no systems in place to allow eBay customers to keep pace with Guernsey's traditional bidders. The plan itself appeared to shut would-be eBay buyers out of any opportunity but to establish a floor bid. Still, Moriarty and company moved ahead with their plans.

"We're just happy to be involved," Moriarty said. "Whoever buys these balls, however they buy them, we come out ahead."

Letter to Mark McGwire from Philip Ozersky, dated December 21, 1998:

"Dear Mr. McGwire:

"Happy Holidays! By way of introduction, I am Philip Ozersky, the fan who was the lucky recipient of your magical 70th home run ball. I would like to thank you as a baseball fan for your wonderful contribution to the 1998 major league season, and congratulate you on the illustrious 70 home run mark you achieved.

"You have touched my life greatly with that last monumental swing of the bat. I want to personally thank you for the excitement and joy it has brought me and those around me; it is certainly a new twist in the life of this research scientist!

"I have decided to sell the ball January 12 at auction in New York, as you may know, and it is my hope that you respect my choice. As not only a Cardinals fan but also an avid baseball fan, it was a very difficult decision for me not to return the ball. However, I could not overlook the effect the sale of this baseball may have on the lives of me and my family.

"The speculation on what the ball might sell for is astonishing and I turn to you as a role model of how to handle myself in this situation. I perceive you as a loving father, consummate professional, and an inspiring philanthropist. I know the money this baseball brings cannot alone buy happiness, but it will dramatically increase my freedom:

- to invest a lot of time in my future children's upbringing
- to help my parents retire
- to allow me the financial stability to remain at a job I love
- to touch countless others by way of charitable contributions

"I hope the 70th ball will be remembered and admired not only as a symbol of your greatness and achievement of '98, but also for the greater good that it will be providing for myself, my family, and countless others. Thanks again for this once-in-a-lifetime opportunity! I hope someday to have the honor of talking with you, shaking your hand, and thanking you personally.

"Sincerely, Philip Ozersky."

Ten

Perhaps the Best Day of All in the Life of a Research Scientist

January 12, 1999

It comes to this.

One hundred and seven days after he grabbed his prize, Philip Ozersky waits for the hours to crawl the length of afternoon to seven o'clock. He passes the time granting interviews to news organizations he has never heard of, for accounts he will never read, see, or hear.

A *Daily News* writer, off his usual beat, wonders if McGwire's historic home run at Busch Stadium was hit in the bottom of the seventh inning or the top.

A Fox News reporter flashes a fresh $50 bill and offers to buy the ball from Ozersky right there on the air, cash money, a straight, clean deal. (Earlier, when this particular *schtick* occurred to the reporter, he could be seen thumbing his wallet for a big enough bill to prop up the joke.)

Ozersky, wearing a necktie decorated with the double helix of a strand of DNA, attempts to answer the questions a little differently each time out, all the while trying not to focus on the knot in his stomach, the uncertainty in his head, the press of well-wishes from his gathered family and friends. He has been looking forward to this moment for months, but he would like to put it off.

Ozersky doesn't know this, but his gathered siblings have chipped in for a personalized long-sleeve shirt they mean to give him later tonight, with the phrase "I used to own Mark McGwire's 70th Home Run Ball" stitched to the front, and beneath the anticipated laugh there is an embroidered truth. In just 107 days, on some visceral level, the ball has come to define Philip Ozersky. It has rewritten the story of his life. He had been branded by it, in fundamental ways that cut deeper than any amount of money it may fetch later on today. He is the guy who caught the ball, the guy who kept the ball, the guy who is selling the ball, the guy who in so doing might change the ways in which we remember the game itself. Here on in, Ozersky will be defined in the negative, known for what he no longer has.

(Many a deep truth has been stitched to a personalized shirt in jest.)

Between interviews, Ozersky busies himself collecting the signatures of his fellow consignors, and posing for pictures. He is, by nature, a fan, but there is also this: In the letting go there is the tendency to reclaim pieces of what we will no longer have. There must be some research to support this phenomenon. They're all doing it: Grass, Kuhlemeier, Chapa, Singer, Wiseman. . . . It started as a way to kill the time, and it's spread. They've even gone outside, these record ball holders, to the Sports Authority on Seventh Avenue, and bought out the few remaining Rawlings Official National League baseballs, and they're collecting signature on these as well. They've posed for pictures alongside a plaque of Mickey Mantle in front of the midtown restaurant that bears the name of the Yankee legend, after a Guernsey's-sponsored luncheon in their honor.

Back in the Madison Square Garden theater lobby, a young woman looks on at all this signing and snapshotting and wonders at who these good and famous people might be. They're being interviewed and signing autographs and flashing smiles. Surely they must be *somebody*.

"Well, yes," the young woman is told. "They're the young fellows who caught the home run balls. This one right there, he caught McGwire's 67th."

"And they're giving each other autographs?" the young woman wonders. "What's that?"

The consignors are like high school seniors, hurrying to fill each other's yearbooks with as much shared history and silliness as they can think up with pen in hand and gun to head. It is a sweet scene but also a shade sad. These good and momentarily famous people are linked by having been in different right places at different right times, connected by their resulting bump and grinds with baseball history. And—oh, yeah!—they all have the same agent, who has got his own set of hastily bought baseballs making the rounds of his clients.

There aren't enough Sharpie extra-fine-point markers to go around.

Guernsey's Arlan Ettinger looks up from the details of these final hours and wonders what craziness he has wrought. There are about a dozen news crews setting up for tonight's sale, their cameras pointed at the signed bats and balls at the curl of the theater lobby, and yet Ozersky and the others move about like the stars of the show.

In a way, they are, but that's not the point. The point, for Ettinger, is that the focus is off. Ettinger's helmed dozens of auctions in his career—estate sales, prized collections, in one case the entire contents of the SS *United States* cruise liner—and he's never seen anything like this. Consignors behaving like celebrities, strong-arming him from his commission, dictating what items he can sell, signing each other's catalogues, troubling his staff with travel arrangements and hotel reservations. Ozersky alone has brought nearly twenty people into town, Ettinger's lost count, and he says his small staff has felt the strain of seeing them here. When someone wants to change a flight, it's forty-five minutes on the phone for one of his people. They want to know where to eat dinner, what shows to see, what sights not to miss. He can understand the excitement, but he's trying to stage an auction here, not a family reunion.

Ettinger would never presume to compare what he does for a living to, say, what a surgeon does, but if you fly into another city for a special procedure your family doesn't start asking the doctor where to stay when they're visiting the hospital. It's all a little ridiculous. And expensive. By contract, he's committed to paying $550 in travel expenses for each of Barnes's clients, plus one night each at the Gramercy Park Hotel (at $170 per), and the nickels and dimes seem to rub out the dollar signs in his eyes. Plus, he's got that big luncheon bill to pay at Mickey Mantle's, and the meter's running on a months-long public relations effort at Rubenstein Public Relations, one of the biggest (and most expensive) press agencies in the city. At times, he appears so concerned with the money going out for expenses, and the commission negotiated away to win Ozersky's consignment, that he can see his dreamed-about payday whittled to nothing.

Just yesterday, Ettinger cornered Ozersky for his third or fourth whispered conversation about a selling bonus. He did this after three or four similar appeals to Freedland, all of which were deflected. Freedland's strategy, it appeared, was to put Ettinger off until the last minute, and then to put him off some more, but Ettinger was persistent. It was the same persistence that won him Ozersky's business, only now it was redirected. Apparently, in the registration of bidders, he had begun to realize that the ball could sell for a far heftier sum than anyone had wildly imagined. By Monday, two dozen bidders had been precertified at the $1 million level. Another half dozen had clearance up to $3 million. Two buyers had established credit lines up to $50 million, and at least one had an authorization to write a blank check.

Ozersky saw the clearance forms himself. Michael Freedland had heard that one high-end bidder from Florida with an unlimited line of credit wanted to buy the ball for his grandson. Mike Barnes knew one of his private bidders had authorization from his investors to pass $5 million. The Guernsey's phone bank at the semicircled rear of the theater lobby hummed with the news that Donald Trump had registered to bid. Ted Turner was said to be participating through a proxy, ostensibly on the Hank Aaron ball. The Topps Baseball Card company was expected to attend, and so were representatives from the Fiesta casino and hotel operation, and Salvino's, makers of the Bamm Beanos bean-filled toys. *Spawn* creator Todd McFarlane, foiled in his private bid for all but the 69th home run ball, would be on one of the Guernsey's telephones. The actor Alec Baldwin was rumored to be planning a run on at least one item, while the actor Charlie Sheen, the man who held the distinction of having paid more money than anyone else for a baseball going into the record-setting 1998 season, was also said to be bidding.

Everyone in attendance has got money on their minds. Most agree that the ball will sell for more than $1 million, but beyond that number no one can say for certain. There has been published speculation that the ball might sell for between $5 and $7 million. The phrase "as much as $10 million" has appeared in several newspaper accounts chronicling the sale. Ozersky's brother-in-law, Brian Button, had a dream in which the number $7.3 million figured prominently. There are office pools and side bets all over the country. Here in the Madison Square Garden lobby, Miles Standish of Professional Sports Authenticators has $1 wagers with collectors Steve Ryan and Mark Lewis that the ball will sell for more than $3 million. At the genome lab on the Washington University campus in St. Louis, the smart money is on or around $2 million. Ozersky's sister Sharon has been working the Madison

Square Garden Theater lobby with a video camera, asking friends, family members, and others involved in the auction to make their predictions. As a goof, one family friend told a Rubenstein executive there was an over-under line out of Vegas on the amount of the sale, who in turn passed the information on to a reporter, which in turn led to speculation on whether the comment would find its way into print.

With all this excitement, Ettinger suggested to Ozersky, don't you think Guernsey's should be rewarded?

Well, yeah, figured Ozersky, but the reward would come in the form of the buyer's premium, as agreed. Not the seller's. Plus, there were now 41 items in the auction—that should yield reward enough, a kind of bonus by association. Wasn't that the pitch that Ettinger himself had made? A Jim Thorpe autographed baseball, lot #25, wasn't even a home run ball. The theme of the auction—the home run balls of 1998—has metastasized to include the kinds of items you can find on the Home Shopping Network: a Waterford Crystal 1998 World Series trophy baseball, lot #41, a commemorative Hall of Fame bat signed by forty-three Hall of Famers, lot #40.

Ettinger can't see how a seller like Ozersky would *not* want to reward him for a job well done. Guernsey's little touches and extra efforts seem about to pay off. Ettinger's not one to count his chickens, because the few times he's done so less than good things have tended to happen, but every indication has been that this sale will be a success. He's reached out to the right people, pushed the right buttons, put the right kind of flourish on what he's taken to calling the most significant auction in sports history. You wouldn't put a ball like Ozersky's in a $3 plastic cube like they do at Christie's. You wouldn't take a Picasso painting to K-Mart and get a $20 picture frame for it. Why demean the ball in the same way? That's why he went out and had these special glass boxes designed to showcase these balls. Not just Ozersky's ball, but all the balls. No other auction house does that. Nobody brings in Donald Trump to their press conferences, let alone as a possible bidder. No other auction house gets this kind of attention for their unusual, one-of-a-kind sales. And what about the catalogue? Do you know how many strings he had to pull to get that thing written and printed in just a few days?

The way Ettinger thinks of it is he's caught in a vice. He's honored he was chosen to handle the sale, and he's committed to doing a good job of it, but he worries if he's reached a point of diminishing returns. The rent on the theater at the Garden alone is running him about five thousand dollars a day, for three days, but realistically it will come to three to four times that amount when he factors in related costs. Madison Square Garden is a union venue, and it runs Guernsey's a small fortune every time Ettinger has a chair moved, or a table. Then there's the cost of all the phone lines, and the round-the-clock security. The Garden provides its own uniformed guards as part of the deal, but Ettinger's got his regular crew on top of that, and his people stay the night.

Sotheby's and Christie's, they're like a Wal-Mart and a K-Mart in a small town. They're like two gas stations on opposite corners. They can keep cutting their prices and cutting their prices, even if it hurts. They can lose money on a sale and still come out ahead because they can take away a chunk of business from their competition, but Ettinger can't afford to do that. This time, it was necessary to waive his seller's commission in order to get the business. Ozersky's people were really tough—Ettinger told the *New York Times* that negotiations to secure selling rights to the ball were "brutal"—but now he would like to have back some of what he's given away.

He's got a figure in mind: five percent for everything over $2 million. Even that wouldn't begin to cover it, but at least it's something.

Beneath the back-and-forth on a selling bonus, there are separate dramas unfolding at slow speed. Most significantly, perhaps, is whether Hank Aaron, baseball's all-time home run king, will show to promote the sale of his final home run ball.

Richard Arndt, for the time being the owner of Hank Aaron's 755th home run ball, isn't counting on it. Arndt's saga has grown famous in the hobby, for the way it pitted the mighty baseball club against the lowly grounds-keeper. In 1976, the Milwaukee Brewers had made it something of a tradition to gift back to Aaron as many of his record-setting home run balls as they could get their hands on, and the team equipment manager cornered Arndt soon after he collected the ball and asked him to return it. If he did so, immediately, the equipment manager would arrange for Aaron to sign another baseball in exchange. Arndt asked if it would be possible to give the ball directly to Aaron, who had been a hero of his back when he played for the Milwaukee Braves. Such a thing would have meant far more to Arndt than a signed baseball delivered through an emissary.

Arndt went home that evening thinking he would meet Aaron at the park the next day and present him with the baseball. At the time, no one knew that 755 would be Aaron's last home run (there were another two and a half months to go in the season), but it would certainly stand as the all-time record until he hit another. However, the next morning, instead of meeting Aaron, Arndt was fired for leaving Milwaukee County Stadium with stolen property. The Brewers deducted $5 from his final paycheck, to pay for the cost of the ball. Arndt put the ball in a safety deposit box and found a new job.

From time to time, over the next nineteen years, Arndt would go to the bank and check on his ball. It was almost like going to a kennel, to visit a pet you had to give up for house-breaking reasons. He'd take pictures. He'd bring friends. He'd move the ball to a new bank, whenever his prospects took him elsewhere. Early on, he received an offer from Magnavox, the electronics company, which had hired Aaron to make promotional visits to dealerships around the country. They were willing to pay $1,000 for the ball, but Arndt turned them down. Every year or so, he'd hear from one of Aaron's representatives, offering to buy the ball directly. Aaron even acknowledged these appeals in his autobiography *I Had a Hammer,* published in 1991. "I've offered him as much as $10,000," he wrote of Arndt, "but he won't part with it. To me, that ball is just as important as the one from number 715, because it's the one that established the record. The record is 755, not 715."

As recently as 1997, Aaron's wife Billye contacted Arndt and offered $30,000 for the ball, which she reportedly intended to present to her husband for his birthday, but he still wouldn't sell.

In 1995, Arndt removed the ball from the bank near his new home in Albuquerque, New Mexico and traveled with it to Phoenix, Arizona, where Aaron was slated to appear at a baseball card and memorabilia show. For $15,

Arndt was allowed to stand in line and ask Aaron to sign the ball. Waiting, he thought about telling Aaron who he was, and what ball he was signing, but then he thought about all the other people in line behind him, and the promoter who went to a lot of trouble to bring Aaron into town. He didn't know how Aaron would react to seeing him, and he didn't want to make a scene, or spoil anybody else's plans for the day, so he waited his turn anonymously and secured Aaron's signature on the ball without comment.

Now, Arndt is taking advantage of the excitement in the sports collectibles market and selling the ball—only Aaron seems to be interfering. According to Arndt, Aaron's representatives talked of publicly questioning the authenticity of his ball unless he agreed to share the proceeds with Aaron's "Chasing the Dream" foundation, in exchange for which the most prolific home run hitter in baseball history would endorse the sale. After weighing the situation in his mind, Arndt agreed to earmark 42.5 percent of the sale to Aaron's foundation, and Aaron agreed to back off. His representatives even suggested the home run king might attend the auction, to stimulate interest in the ball and shine a light on his charitable work. Arlan Ettinger confirms these developments, but he does not want the Hall of Famer to be seen in a negative light; rather, he suggests that Aaron's camp was prepared to challenge Arndt's right to sell the ball, not whether the ball itself was legitimate.

Either way, this much seems clear: Arndt feels strong-armed into accepting Aaron's terms, despite the impeccable provenance on his ball. If ever there was a well-documented piece of baseball history, Arndt's ball surely qualifies. The man travels with a loose-leaf binder stuffed with clippings and correspondence, chronicling his life with the ball. He even keeps pink While You Were Out message slips, as a record of the telephone conversations he's had about the ball, and those records show that the last direct contact he had with Aaron came during spring training in 1986. Aaron just picked up the phone and called Arndt at his new home in Albuquerque and told him once more that he was interested in buying the ball. A few months later, Arndt heard from a person in Westchester County, New York, who identified herself as Aaron's agent and attempted to persuade Arndt that his ball had gone down in value since 1976, and that his best offer would likely come from Aaron himself. "She made a point of saying how Aaron didn't play in a big city like New York or Chicago," Arndt recalls, "and that the ball was hit ten years ago. She even suggested that one of the reasons the ball had depreciated was because Aaron was black. I thought, 'Well, that's interesting.' I'd never heard of a collectible like this losing value, and then she told me she thought it was worth about five thousand dollars. So that was the end of that conversation."

Arndt is a circumspect man who seems to care deeply about the game of baseball and the city of Milwaukee. In conversation, he speaks frequently about the debt he owes to each. He even speaks glowingly of Aaron, one of his boyhood heroes. "That's the irony of this whole situation," he says. "I grew up watching the Milwaukee Braves. If Aaron had just taken the time to sit down with me, in his uniform, the night he hit the home run, or maybe some time later, chances are I would have given him the ball. Just given it to him. And now . . ."

His voice trails off, and he realizes how he's made Aaron look with his version of the events leading up to

tonight's sale. "If someone comes out of this story looking like a bad guy," he corrects himself, "I'd rather it be
me than Hank Aaron. He's an icon, I don't want to criti-
cize him, but I kind of got hammered into going along
with this agreement. To give up forty-two and a half percent of the proceeds, that's an awful lot. And for what?
Probably nothing. He's not going to show. His blessing or
endorsement is probably not going to amount to much. I
don't want to create a problem for anybody, and I don't
want to say anything against Hank Aaron, but I felt this
whole thing wasn't handled very ethically. I felt, for a
couple days, I had a gun in my ribs. I'm giving this away
out of the kindness of my heart, is really the bottom line.

"I'm never gonna get any Christmas cards from Hank
Aaron, and I'm not looking for any, but I think he should
feel grateful that I didn't sell the ball, I didn't use it or
abuse or mistreat it. I've kept it in a safe place, and I've
been honest. I've tried to get it back to the Brewers, and
they wouldn't even respond to us. It shouldn't be sitting
in my safety deposit box. It's bigger than that. There's a
lot of history to this ball, and I think the right place for
it is either in the Hall of Fame, or in Milwaukee County
Stadium, for people to see. I just feel like I should be
compensated for all the time I've spent with the ball, for
everything I've done."

Specifically, he feels he should be compensated with
at least $465,000. That would be his take if the ball
meets its reserve price of $850,000, less 5 percent seller's
commission.

"I might make a fool of myself tonight," he says,
"but if the ball doesn't go for $850,000, I might just walk
away from it."

* * *

At four-thirty this afternoon, a photographer is dispatched to the Madison Square Garden Theater lobby to take a picture of the McGwire ball for a book cover. For two days now, the ball has sat for thousands of pictures under Guernsey's custom glass cubes, but its smile is waning. Most news agencies are anxious to get another angle on the ball, a shot that doesn't look like everyone else's, but the consignor and the consignee can't possibly honor every request for special treatment. The insurance rider taken to cover the auction and public viewing does not allow for the ball to be handled any more than necessary, but Ozersky has given his word that the publisher can take an open-air photo of the ball, so arrangements are made.

Guernsey's instructs the photographer assigned to the shoot, Brad Wilson, to set up in a hallway adjacent to the theater lobby, using a store-bought Rawlings baseball to adjust the lighting. The idea, as much as possible, is to limit the amount of time the ball is out from under its case. Ettinger, himself a photographer, bellows that he could set and light this shot in twenty seconds—it is, merely, a still life of a round object—and he tells his people to pull the ball if it takes any longer than a few minutes. He doesn't understand why this couldn't have been done earlier.

A television cameraman stands back a couple paces, recording the slapped-together scene.

When the shot is framed, and lit, the "real" ball will be escorted to the hallway by two security guards, Ozersky's attorney Michael Freedland, and Guernsey's representative Scott Knauer. It seems like an awful lot of people, to babysit a baseball—but these are no ordinary people, and this is no ordinary baseball. Knauer and security chief Ty Yorio have been instructed to wear white gloves while handling the ball, which arrives on the makeshift set a moment ahead of schedule. Wilson and his long-haired assistant, Magnus Lanje, hurry to complete their preparations. Their plan, oddly, is to hold the ball in place with a piece of tape, but this will clearly not do. This might have occurred to the photographers, who otherwise appear to be doing a professional job of things, on terrifically short notice. That is, it might have occurred to them if they had any idea how obsessive grown people can be when it comes to their extraordinary baseballs.

"It's not a toy," Yorio explains to the photographer, with the kind of disdain most people hold in reserve for conversations with child molestors.

PSA's Miles Standish is summoned to consult on the ball-tape problem, and he quickly agrees that the tape is an unacceptable solution. Quickly, he jerry rigs a way for the round ball to remain still on the flat surface, and Lanje gets his cue to remove the store-bought stand-in from the shot to make way for the genuine article. He does this without much thought—apparently, with not nearly enough thought to suit the ball's bodyguards.

"Lose the ball," Ty Yorio mumbles under his breath to Lanje, the photographer's assistant, as the real ball is put in its place on the table.

Lanje looks back at this man and wonders if he's talking to him.

"Lose the ball," Yorio says again, this time as if he's auditioning for Scorsese. Truly, his voice is so thick with distrust for this long-haired, fake-baseball-holding menace that the collar on his already tight-fitting turtleneck might split from the tension in his throat.

"What?" Lange responds, innocently enough. "Me?"

Rather than make himself clear, Yorio chooses to repeat himself. "Lose the ball." He speaks into his chest, in a manner that suggests what he'd really rather be doing for a living is guarding presidents.

Lanje holds out the ball. "This?" he says.

"Put it in your pocket," Yorio insists, improvising.

Presumably, the concern Yorio means to convey is that the store-bought ball can too easily be mistaken for the McGwire ball and that he is uncomfortable having the two in such close proximity to each other, in such a crowded room. It would be far too simple for someone to make a switch, and if Ty Yorio and his people at Citadel Security are not on their toes it might be a minute or two before anyone notices. Citadel has been working Guernsey's auctions since they were dealing cigars and comic books, and Yorio is not about to let a couple of pissant photographers cost him the account.

Lanje finally gets past Yorio's limited powers of communication and puts the ball in his pocket. He seems to shrug, as if, all along, what he meant to do was swap balls and make a run for it, down the escalator to Seventh Avenue.

He's never seen such a lot of fuss over a baseball.

Eric Moriarty does not appear too happy. The on-line preauction has not gone well. A visit to eBay's site reveals only one bid on McGwire's 70th home run ball—at $100,000—and no action on any of the other items.

One bid!

It seems hardly worth the expense and effort, and yet here they are, a half-dozen eBay people, and their public relations team, and all of their supporting hardware and bells and whistles. They've even flown in a young woman from the company's San Jose offices named Lisa Laursen, whose assignment it will be to log in the bidding in as close to real time as her fingers can manage. Laursen, a customer support technician from Gilroy, California, "The Garlic Capital of the World," worries before the auction if her typing skills will be swift enough to keep pace with the call of auctioneer Joane Grant, but an onlooker gets the sense that this is the least of eBay's concerns. They just hope there's someone on the other end of their screens, trying to get in on the bidding.

At 7 P.M. there are fifty-four press units assembled about the Madison Square Garden Theater lobby. These include local, network, and cable news crews, some of which plan to cut-in live to regular programming to cover the sale of the 70th home run ball. There is also a phalanx of print reporters and photographers, including representatives from news agencies in Japan, Germany, Australia, Mexico, Puerto Rico, and Canada.

In the hastily expanded seating area in front of the podium, there are about four hundred mostly business-suited men and women. Mark Lewis, one of several dozen memorabilia dealers in attendance, sits in the front row and swears he can sniff the money in the room. "See that guy," he says, pointing to a well-dressed middle-aged man who crosses his path. "There's ten million dollars right there. I don't know that man, I don't know who he is or why he's here, but he's got money."

Across the aisle, also in the front row, sits Arthur T. Shorin, president of Topps Baseball Card company, who means to make a run at Ozersky's ball. His notion is to insert a special ticket into one of his 1999 baseball card packs and give one lucky boy or girl the thrill of catching the ball. He's thinking just over $1 million will be what it takes. Anything more than $1.3 million will surprise the hell out of him.

Sara Wight, a roommate of Guernsey's associate Amye Austin, waits by the bank of phones at the front of the room, facing the crowd, as in a telethon. She'll be seated to the auctioneer's far left, phone to her ear, with an absentee bidder on the line. No one will know the bidder's identity but Wight, Ettinger, and certain members of Guernsey's staff.

Ozersky claims his seat in what was once the fourth row but is now the seventh, after the Madison Square Garden crew rushed another three rows of folding chairs to the front of the room to accommodate the crowd. He sits on the aisle, anchoring a long row of family and friends, which also includes Michael Freedland and David Krathen. Around him, here and there, sit his fellow consignors. John Grass and his entourage, two rows down; Vern Kuhlemeier and "the wife," off to the left of the room, facing front; Richard Arndt, with his wife and son, in the middle of the fourth row. Mike Barnes and Miles Standish sit with their wives on the aisle seats, two rows in front of the Ozersky assemblage. In all there seems to be more people connected in one way or another to the consignors than there are people expecting in one way or another to take home one of the items up for sale.

7:15 P.M. Ettinger steps to the podium in front of the packed house and says this: "I think without argument, the most significant baseball in the world today, it sits to my right. Mark McGwire's 70th ball. There's nothing I can really say that would do it justice, so we'll just skip the color commentary on it and go for it."

Auctioneer Joane Grant, a round-faced woman with matching round glasses, opens the bidding at $500,000, and then for some reason dips to $400,000. No mention is made of any leading eBay bid. She fishes for about ten seconds until someone finally takes the bait, and then they're off. Initially, the bidding moves swiftly, in $50,000 increments, almost without pause. The bidding is pushed along, as it is in most auctions, by anonymous representatives of the auction house itself, who have no intention of buying the baseball. It is not known how many such bidders are in attendance, or who they are, but they are certainly here.

"Bidding off the back wall," as it is known in the trade, allows an auction house to develop a bidding velocity, up to the unpublished minimum reserve price. The practice is legal in most states, including New York, and accounts for the fact that a disproportionate number of items sell at precisely their minimum reserves. Technically, it is a violation of the consignment contract for an auction house to bid on one of its items, but a bid beneath the minimum is not considered an *actual* bid because the item is not available for sale at that low price. The strategy works like this: When only one genuine bidder is interested in an item, the planted bidder will drop out at just below the minimum, leaving the item available to the one interested party at the lowest price the consignor has agreed to accept. In most instances, consignors and bona fide bidders are unaware of the charade.

Here, with a little help from Guernsey's plants, the bidding reaches $1 million after just one minute and four seconds. The bidders seem to raise their paddles without thinking, possibly knowing that at these lower levels they won't be stuck having to pay for the item at the close of the sale. Still, it's a sweat-on-the-brow moment, to publicly pledge that kind of money for a simple baseball, and if they're raising their paddles without much thought they're also putting them down wondering what the hell they've just done.

Topps' Shorin raised his paddle at $1.2 million, thinking perhaps he will come in $100,000 shy of blowing his own mind, although with the buyer's premium his bid represents a commitment of $1.374 million of his company's funds. He is quickly rolled by a $1.25 million bid from the back of the room, and he places his paddle at his side, where it will remain for the rest of the auction.

The bidding stalls at $1.35 million, owing possibly to the fact that the Guernsey's back wall bidders dropped out once Ozersky's $1.25 million minimum reserve was reached. The pause runs a full thirty seconds, during which Grant eyeballs her previous bidders and coaxes them further. "Any advance?" she says, stretching. "Fair warning, then." Just before she closes out the bidding, Sara Wight raises her hand with a $1.4 million bid from the phone, one beat ahead of the gavel.

Later, Wight's absentee bidder will tell how he and Wight had worked out a system. She would report the standing bid, and if he was interested in advancing he would say, "Please." The problem with this system, the absentee bidder joked, was that as the bidding intensified and he grew more astonished at the money involved, Wight invariably mistook his plaintive cries of "Jeez!" for an advance.

From here, the bidding accelerates, and at $1.5 million begins to move in $100,000 increments. Soon, the active bidders in attendance fall away, save for tie manufacturer Irwin Sternberg, who is seated in the back of the

but he found it difficult to bid against an opponent he could not see; for all he knew, the guy had a bottomless pit full of money. Sometime later, the anonymous guy on the telephone will respond that his pit was not in fact bottomless, although he did have one more bid left in him. That's all.

Grant closes the bidding after eight minutes and two seconds, and awards the ball to the telephone bidder for $2.7 million. With the buyer's premium, it represents a $3.005 million pledge, a figure which will be mistakenly reported by almost every major news organization later this evening and the following morning as $3.05 million.

Topps' Shorin stands to leave.

Ettinger steps to the microphone and holds out his hands to quiet the room. "In the words of the late Mel Allen," he quips, " 'How about that?' "

Mike Barnes's other clients don't have long to wait for the first sign of trouble. Guernsey's strategy is to bunch the McGwire and Sosa record home run balls at the top of the auction, and sprinkle its other marquee items—Hank Aaron's 755th home run ball and Mickey Mantle's 500th—throughout the sale.

The second item up for bid, Sammy Sosa's 61st home run ball, with the proceeds going to the slugger's charitable foundation, commands an undersized $15,000, from Sara Wight's anonymous telephone bidder.

Next, McGwire's 63rd home run ball is called, and when the bidding opens at $10,000, consignor John Grass is apoplectic. He doesn't understand how an item with a $50,000 minimum reserve doesn't open at $50,000. That's not how it was explained to him. He would never have agreed to the sale if he knew they were going to start it so low. Psychologically, you can't put such a cheap price on an item and expect it to sell for big bucks. He sits and fidgets and fumes, as his ball slowly climbs in value. When the bidding stops at $32,000, Grass turns to his buddy Larry Thomas and says, "It's not possible." He had turned down $200,000 from McFarlane, thinking he could do better at auction, and here they actually stop the auction at $32,000. It doesn't make any sense. Grant momentarily withdraws the lot for failing to meet its reserve, but Ettinger jumps toward the podium to announce a bid in the back of the room. With this, the bidding gets going again, back and forth between the telephone and the bidders on the back wall.

The winning telephone bid is exactly $50,000, and it's all John Grass can do to keep himself from charging the podium and throttling Arlan Ettinger.

Lot #4, Sosa's 64th home run ball, opens at $20,000, and Grass is even more incensed. Why does Vern's ball open at $20,000 and mine at $10,000? he wonders. He doesn't get it. Grass's ball at least set a record; Vern's is just one of many. Apparently, the assembled collectors agree, because the bidding only reaches $24,000, and the lot passes. Vern Kuhlemeier smiles like he doesn't know what just happened.

Albert Chapa's 66th Sosa ball, with a $150,000 reserve, opens at $50,000 and moves slowly to $55,000, at which point Grant cancels the lot. Some in the crowd mumble that she is too quick with the gavel, not giving bidders enough time to organize their strategies. Just then, once again, Ettinger points out a bid his auctioneer seems to have missed, and the bidding gets rolling again toward the minimum, which it manages to reach precisely, thanks to the same anonymous guy on the phone.

The mood of the room, which had moments ago been exuberant, is now somber and stunned. None of those involved in the auction expected to move from such highs to such lows in such a short space of time. McGwire's 67th home run ball sells for $50,000, its minimum, to Sara Wight's telephone bidder; the 68th ball sells for $50,000, also its minimum, also to the telephone.

Mike Barnes looks like someone put a match to his business.

Moments later, when Grant reaches the Mickey Mantle ball, lot #20, there's a rumbling at the back of the room that quickly makes its way to the front. It's accompanied by Bill Edelman, proprietor of Mickey Mantle's restaurant on Central Park South, who in turn is accompanied by the widow of the Yankee great on a cellular telephone. Mrs. Mantle, at the eleventh hour and fifty-ninth minute, has called to contest the authenticity of her late husband's 500th home run ball, which she claims to have in her possession. Ettinger pulls the item from the sale and is nearly booed from the podium by several dozen collectors who had planned to bid. "A question has come up," he hastily explains. "We don't want to sell something that has a question. You think I don't want to sell it to you? Please."

Ever since the extraordinary sale of the 70th home run ball, the auction hasn't gone well, and Barnes and Freedland wonder if Ettinger thinks he can move the ball for a higher price at a later date. It also occurs to them, without knowing of the cellular phone call, that there might be a legitimate claim against the ball. Mantle's widow is well known in the hobby for contesting the sale of certain of her husband's items as they go to auction.

The Aaron ball, lot #37, rolls around a short time

later, and here again Ozersky stands to collect half of Ettinger's fee. Surely, he thinks, this ball will do better than some of the other balls. This is a monumental record, 755 career home runs. As an achievement, it's possibly a bigger deal than McGwire's 70 home runs in a single season. Ettinger is inclined to agree, and he tells the assembled bidders that the ball should be considered in the same light as the record McGwire ball. "Very proudly," Ettinger says, "we're able to announce that almost half the proceeds will be going to the Henry Aaron Chasing the Dream foundation, a foundation Mr. Aaron fervently believes in. We have his blessings in the sale of this ball." He fails to mention that Aaron was expected to show, or that his blessings cost Richard Arndt 42.5 percent of the eventual sale price.

Grant opens the bidding at $500,000, but with no takers she drops to $300,000, at which point the bidding moves in fits and starts. When it stops, at $750,000, Ettinger approaches the microphone and reminds the audience that 42.5 percent of the sale price will go to Aaron's foundation, as if this might shake another $100,000 from some unsuspecting buyer. But there is no further interest in the item, and it goes unsold.

After the auction, Ettinger pulls tie manufacturer Irwin Sternberg from a press interview in the theater lobby and tries to turn him into a buyer of the Aaron ball.

"I saw you raise your paddle," Ettinger starts in, "and if you're still interested I thought we could maybe get together with the seller and try to work something out."

Sternberg is flummoxed. He never bid on the Aaron ball. He did spend $69,000 on a ball signed by Babe Ruth and Roger Maris, to which he hopes to add Mark McGwire's signature, but he couldn't see any marketing possibilities in the Aaron ball. In his view, the Ruth and Maris ball, like the McGwire ball, is a great national treasure—and an inspiration to young people all around the country. It ties in to Jimmy V's message: *Never give up.* The Aaron ball never even figured into his company's thinking.

Nevertheless, Ettinger is anxious to make a sale, and Sternberg has shown himself as a buyer. If Richard Arndt could be persuaded to sell his ball to the high bidder for $750,000, Guernsey's would collect an additional $150,000, which it would have to split with Ozersky under the terms of his consignment agreement. An additional $75,000, with the disappointing proceeds from those "lesser" balls, would go a long way toward shoring up the auction house's bottom line.

"So," Ettinger tries, one final time, "it's not something you want to consider, then?"

Overheard:

One collector, speculating to another on why they've yet to see any of the bases or resin bags or other items from the final game at Busch Stadium. Their shared thinking is that Cardinals' owner Bill DeWitt Jr., a known hobbyist with a major collection of baseball memorabilia and artifacts, is hoarding the items for himself.

"Nothing leaves Busch Stadium," one says to the other.

"He's got his guys, they go in there, right after a game, they lock everything up," the other bemoans, as if perhaps DeWitt should be expected to do otherwise. As if the owner of the St. Louis Cardinals, the man who pays for all this stuff in the first place, has an obligation to those in the hobby to let at least a few items slip through his grasp.

* * *

John Grass is rabid. He rushes at Arlan Ettinger during a postauction press conference—not to hurt him, necessarily, but to express his disdain. "You lied to me!" Grass hollers. "You didn't deal with me straight."

Ettinger, working the microphones and basking in the positive attention of the $3.005 million sale on the 70th home run ball, doesn't notice the tirade.

"I believe in being a man of your word," Grass reflects, after some deep breathing. "I was told the bidding would start at $50,000. Every one of these guys, we were told $50,000. It didn't happen that way. I don't know if it's in my contract or anything, but I don't give a rat's ass. If he lied to me, he lied to me. It just pisses me off. If they had started at $50,000 and that's all I got, I'm happy as a lark. But if they'd have started mine at $50,000, it would have gone higher. That guy on the phone, he would have been up to it. And everyone else was affected by how mine ended up doing.

"We had these quarter million dollar offers when we all turned down McFarlane, and now we're getting screwed."

Two hours later, Grass has mellowed. He's still sour, but he's not about to wring anyone's neck. He and his son and his buddies have inhaled a few steaks and shrimp cocktails, courtesy of Philip Ozersky, and he's resigned himself to what's happened. "Hell," he says, "that's life, buddy." He's civil, and subdued, but what had been his good cheer is not likely to resurface in the next while.

Ozersky has graciously invited his fellow consignors and their families to join his group for a post-auction dinner at Broadway Joe's, a once-popular steakhouse that seems to pull most of its customers from midtown hotel fliers and quarter-page ads placed in *Playbill,* the program guide distributed in Broadway theaters. Ozersky's brother David found one of the restaurant's ads in his hotel, offering a 10 percent discount, and booked the back room for a party of thirty people, thinking it would be a celebration. It is and it isn't. Ozersky's extended family is fairly overjoyed and still somewhat incredulous over the evening's turn of events, while Heath Wiseman, Doug Singer, Albert Chapa, Vern Kuhlemeier, and John Grass can't help but think of what they've missed; they do what they can not to turn the celebration pale.

Ozersky himself is even tempered, and marginally out of sorts. He's had a busy day. He's trying not to think about the money. He'd heard so many outrageous estimates about what the ball might go for—$10 million! someone actually thought it would go for $10 million!— he's careful not to feel disappointed with his take. It registers, and it doesn't. It's so far beyond what he ever hoped to accumulate at this stage in his life that it's hard to comprehend what it means. He's not sure he should even bother to try so soon after what's happened.

When the bill arrives, at the end of the evening, Ozersky doesn't blink. It comes to $1,177, with tax and tip, after adjusting for the discount. It's not only the biggest tab he's ever paid, it's the biggest tab he's ever seen, and he signs off on it as if it's the most natural thing in the world. He considers this, and what gets to him is the fact that, for the moment, it is.

Eleven

Postgame

Or, Still Putting $3.005 Million into Something Resembling Perspective

America Online message to Philip Ozersky, dated January 13, 1998, 9:31 A.M., fourteen hours after Guernsey's Madison Square Garden auction:

"If you're the infamous Philip Ozersky who sold Mark McGwire's 70th home run baseball for $2.7 million, I have one word for you . . . . . LOSER . . . if not, then please accept my apologies for targeting the wrong person.

"The fact that the Philip Ozersky who sold the Mark McGwire baseball would keep the profits from the sale to himself rather than donating the ball to the Hall of Fame and then hiding behind the claim that 'This is America' obviously demonstrates his qualities for this description, loser. This guy could have at least donated a portion of his 'windfall' to some worthy cause, assuming that Philip, if that's you, had a moral fiber to himself.

"You obviously represent the worst elements of professional sports today: individualism, self-gain, self-centeredness, etc., etc. These are the pitfalls which have brought down the purity of baseball and most recently the NBA.

"All I can say to you is this, if you are the same Philip Ozersky: GET A LIFE. If you really believe that you'll have more friends now that you've got some more money to party with, then you obviously are too lame to gain friends on your personal attributes alone.

"Do something decent for the sports world and the rest of us who truly love and respect baseball and at least do something charitable with your new found income.

"A baseball fan."

Phil Ozersky arrived back in St. Louis late Wednesday evening, January 13. He couldn't pick up a newspaper, or turn on the radio, or run into someone he hadn't seen for some time without hearing how his life would now change, but he was still waiting for the transformation. He didn't feel any different. He didn't feel rich. He was the same guy, with the same decisions waiting to be made, the same life to be lived. Three million dollars was a lot, but not enough to reinvent yourself. It was not *fuck you* money. He'd heard the phrase, but never in a way he could apply to his own life, and now it was as if it had been coined with him in mind.

He worked the numbers in his head, and after taking out for taxes, and expenses, and after helping out his folks, and funding his summer camp, Cardinals Care, the

American Cancer Society, and the Leukemia Society of America, he imagines there'll be about $1 million left. It might be more, and it might be less, but he tended to think in round numbers. He tried to imagine the impact that kind of money might have. This wasn't the first time he'd given himself over to such imaginings, but it was the first time they were rooted in real terms.

Mostly, Ozersky started to think, the way the sale of Mark McGwire's 70th home run ball had already changed him was in what it had taken away. Already, his life was no longer his own. He couldn't concentrate at work, couldn't spend uninterrupted time with his friends and family, couldn't sit still and do nothing at all. He moved about as if he had to account for himself. It had been that way since September, true, but the auction reinforced this for him. Everyone seemed to want a piece of him. A figurative piece, a literal piece, whatever.

Even Guernsey's chief Arlan Ettinger wanted his share. This was a man who had pledged his fiduciary responsibility to bring Ozersky the best possible return on his ball, and by outward measures he had done just that. Ozersky confined his thinking to *outward* measures, because he suspected the anonymous buyer was Todd McFarlane, the comic book publisher and toy manufacturer who had been pursuing the ball in a private sale. If that was the case, Ozersky thought, then Ettinger hadn't delivered anything—McFarlane was Mike Barnes's buyer!—and yet he still had his hand out. Ozersky couldn't understand how someone could make a deal, wake up one morning and realize the terms were probably not to his advantage, and call the other party and ask for a do-over. That's essentially what Ettinger was doing. He'd negotiated away his seller's commission, to win the consignment, and now he wanted it back. Five percent of everything over $2 million—or, $35,000. What did he think the ball would sell for? We already had offers of $2 million before we signed to do the auction. It's not like we were hoping he'd bring in a buyer for the ball at some level *lower* than what we had already established.

Ozersky had plenty of time to dwell on things. His flight had been delayed four hours, due to an ice storm. He was the kind of tired where it wasn't quite clear he was thinking straight. Someone recognized him from the television coverage and asked him to sign his copy of *USA Today,* where there was an article about the auction. It was surreal. Even his house looked different to him. Small. Dark. Already, he was thinking where he and Amanda might move, how they'd fix the place up, when they'd be dropped back down, settled, into those new lives people kept talking about. He wondered how he'd ever be able to get back to work, when business as usual might kick in.

He switched on the television set, for the distraction. He flipped channels, looking for something to hold his attention. He might have expected what happened next, but it caught him off guard. He landed on NBC, in time for the *Tonight Show* monologue, and he quickly realized Jay Leno was talking about him. His ball. His auction. Him. Leno wondered why the bidder chose to remain anonymous, and then he punch lined how it was only fitting, seeing how the guy's wife would probably kill him when she found out how he was spending their money. It was a simple, obvious joke, and it pulled the kind of studio audience laughter that had mostly to do with recognition.

Ozersky's own take on the joke was harder to figure.

He didn't care that it was funny, or obvious. He just cared that it was there. It blindsided him that his life had suddenly become material for a guy like Jay Leno. It shouldn't have mattered, or made such a dent in his thinking, but he couldn't set it aside. At this point, he'd been on the *Today* show. Fox News, ESPN, CNN. He'd been interviewed by reporters from *The New York Times, The Washington Post,* and *Sports Illustrated*. He should have been used to it by now, but this felt different than all those other appearances. This was the *Tonight Show*. This was Jay Leno's monologue.

This was a whole other level.

Of the 143 messages waiting for Mike Barnes on his jammed answering machine when he returned to his office Thursday, there was one that jumped to the head of the pile to be returned. It was from the hard-to-reach Judy Smith, a Washington, DC attorney and agent Barnes had been chasing for weeks. Barnes was thinking ahead, to what he might do with his jump-started business once the auction was over, and Smith had something he desperately wanted. Or, she had access to something he desperately wanted: a dress. *The* dress. Monica Lewinsky's presidentially stained dress.

See, Barnes had been thinking the dress could be a centerpiece in a planned impeachment sale. He was learning that in the auction and memorabilia markets, it didn't hurt to have a theme. He was also learning that if he was going to make a living representing inanimate objects, it paid to go after the biggest ones on the block. Think in big, broad strokes. It was his new business plan. Already, he was in discussions with a couple who held an opening day ticket to the 1868 Senate impeachment trial and a gentleman who owned a box of Swisher Sweet brand cigars signed by Bill Clinton in 1992. (Swisher Sweets were the very brand President Clinton "enjoyed" with Ms. Lewinsky, according to her testimony before special prosecutor Ken Starr.) Other items would follow, he felt sure, once he cut a deal with a major auction house—or possibly with eBay, with whom he now had a good working relationship.

For the longest time, Judy Smith would not return Barnes's calls, until he and his clients made headlines. What do you make of that? he thought to himself, dialing her number. Smith, who represented Lewinsky for personal appearances and marketing opportunities, reported that the dress was not yet being shopped in the collectibles market, but she and her client would be happy to consider any proposal Barnes would put forward. The only problem was the dress was being held as evidence by Starr, and it was unclear when, or if, it would be returned to Lewinsky. Once it was, however, she would certainly consider parting with it, for the right price.

Barnes didn't even want to think about the kind of numbers an item like that could bring.

Kerry Woodson, the twenty-two-year-old auto body representative who caught McGwire's 69th home run ball, wouldn't change places with anyone. He's sorry, but he wouldn't be Philip Ozersky for all the money in the world—not even $2.7 million.

"The way everything's happened, I wouldn't change a thing," he said, after selling his ball privately for $200,000 to comic book publisher Todd McFarlane, the man thought to be the anonymous buyer of McGwire's 70th home run ball. "Me, catching it early in the game.

And really catching it. You can see me on the replay. That's something I'll remember for years and years to come."

That last game of the season, going into the late innings, Woodson saw the value of his ball drop seven figures with one swing of the bat, as McGwire's 70th home run left his 69th seeming small by comparison, but Woodson didn't care. He was thrilled to see McGwire reach such a significant new milestone, even if it came at significant cost to him. "People don't believe me when I say that," Woodson explained, "but it's true. I really wouldn't trade places with Ozersky. He's had to change his whole lifestyle. The ball runs his life. People know who he is. I'm very happy being the anonymous 69 guy."

So happy that as part of his private deal with McFarlane, Woodson will make a cameo appearance in an upcoming *Spawn* movie and have a character named for him in the *Spawn* comic book series.

So much for anonymity.

January 19, 1999. One week after the Guernsey's sale, the Concord Resort Hotel was auctioned off for $10.25 million—roughly 3.4 times the amount paid for Ozersky's ball—to a New York real estate group led by hotel developer Joseph Murphy. More than one hundred people crowded into Courtroom 520 at the United States Bankruptcy Court in White Plains, New York, to learn the fate of the famous Catskills hotel, which at one time was a premier "Borscht Belt" destination for wealthy Jewish families. The resort sits on more than 1,700 acres on Kiamesha Lake, less than a two-hour drive from Manhattan, and features forty tennis courts, two skating rinks, two

18-hole golf courses, one 9-hole golf course, indoor and outdoor pools, and skiing and toboggan facilities.

The hotel closed its doors in November 1998, after failing to emerge from Chapter 11 bankruptcy proceedings.

At full occupancy, the Concord had been big enough to accommodate every baseball player from the 1998 opening day rosters of every major league team, along with their families (and, perhaps, their agents and their families, if these people had it in mind to vacation together). And there would have been room left over, in the resort's extensive banquet and conference rooms, to warehouse every professional baseball ever made by the Rawlings Sporting Goods Company.

The bidding, which was delayed nearly three hours to allow Judge Adlai S. Hardin, Jr. to determine the financing of one of the participants, took less than fifteen minutes. After the auction, a spokesperson for Murphy announced plans to renovate the property in conjunction with the Sheraton Hotel chain, at a projected cost of $50 million. The new hotel, the Sheraton Concord Resort Hotel and Convention Center, is expected to open in January 2000.

Guernsey's reported direct catalogue sales of 236 copies—well short of the 100,000 number tossed about in wide-eyed conjecture by Ozersky and his fellow consignors ever since they were offered pieces of the catalogue action as part of their consignment agreements.

In addition, the auction house shipped two thousand non-returnable copies to Amazon.com, which left Ozersky entitled to $11,180 in catalogue royalties. Barnes's other clients, who were to receive a portion of the profits on the catalogue sales, rather than a fixed amount per catalogue, were informed that there were no profits to date and that none were forthcoming.

John Grass fumed about contacting an attorney to explore the possibilities of a lawsuit, either for breach of contract, or fraud, or something.

Executives at eBay attempted to put a positive spin on their mostly disappointing first step into the live auction marketplace and trumpeted the fact that the company had listed for sale seven thousand additional McGwire and Sosa items since the Madison Square Garden auction.

No mention was made of the number of bidders who participated through eBay in the Guernsey's sale.

The St. Louis Cardinals announced that the private party box in left field where Ozersky retrieved the 70th home run ball would be renamed The 70 Suite and refurbished for the 1999 season. New seats will be added, and the room will be redecorated to reflect the site's historical connection to Mark McGwire's historical season.

Naturally, ticket prices for the private room will be affected by the change. During the 1998 season, group rate tickets were $45, which included unlimited beverage service. For 1999, group-rate tickets will be offered at $70, leaving Cardinals fans to wonder how they'll afford to sit in the section where Mark McGwire's 500th career home run ball lands, which it is projected to do sometime during the 1999 season.

Team executives justified the jump in price by pointing out the "value-added" items to be included in the

70 Suite promotional package: a commemorative cap and pin.

January 22, 1999. Todd McFarlane wired $3.005 million to Guernsey's Marine Midland Bank account. His offices had still not publicly confirmed that McFarlane was the buyer of Ozersky's ball, or the half dozen other balls purchased anonymously at the auction, and the man himself was unavailable for comment, but there had been several published accounts linking McFarlane to the sale. His own father unwittingly corroborated the speculation. "Who let the cat out of the bag?" Bob McFarlane responded, when an Associated Press reporter phoned him at his Calgary home.

Privately, however, McFarlane was willing to come clean. He contacted Mike Barnes in St. Louis, acknowledged that the press accounts were accurate, and quietly began negotiations for Sosa's 64th home run ball, which did not meet its reserve price at auction, and McGwire's 64th, which was not included in the sale. He offered $50,000 for each, wanting to complete his collection of in-circulation record balls, but Jason King, the owner of the McGwire ball, rejected the deal. Sosa's ball, owned by Vern Kuhlemeier, was still encumbered by the terms of the Guernsey's agreement, and unavailable for outside sale at the time.

On McFarlane's authority, Barnes contacted Freedland and Ozersky, and told them McFarlane had bought the ball. Ozersky didn't know what to do with this information, except to drive out to his neighborhood Blockbuster and rent the director's cut-version of *Spawn*. He'd spoken to the guy over the phone, and he'd seen his comic books, but now that they were banded by this headline-making transaction, Ozersky figured he should at least watch his movie.

Barnes and Freedland turned their speculations to when Guernsey's would release the funds to Ozersky, now that payment had been made. By contract, Ettinger wasn't required to do so until January 31, a Sunday, and the gap was troubling to Ozersky's representatives for two reasons. First, without cause and principally because they were conditioned to think in worst-case scenarios, they worried that if Guernsey's should for some reason file for bankruptcy before the money was released, Ozersky would become a creditor, and he'd have to take his turn alongside everyone else in dividing up the auction house's assets. McFarlane would have the ball, and Ozersky would be lucky to get 50 cents on the dollar. Second, and more plausibly, they felt the loss of interest income was enough to warrant prompt payment. They turned to their calculators to quantify what the legitimate delay would cost their client. At 5.5 percent, which represented a conservative return on such a substantial investment in a standard money market account, Ozersky's $2.7 million would generate $148,500 a year in interest, or approximately $407 per day.

That's his selling bonus right there, Freedland thought. It's Guernsey's right to hold onto that money, but he'd think Ettinger would release the funds as quickly as possible if he was trying to work another payment out of his client. To Freedland it was the difference between good faith and cunning, between doing the most for your client and doing the least.

Ettinger, when pressed, maintained that he would simply be fulfilling the terms of the contract, by holding onto the money until the agreed-upon date, and pointed out that most auction houses take up to sixty days to relinquish funds to their consignors, sometimes longer.

Even so, Freedland held. Either you negotiate from a position of good faith, or you don't.

January 25, 1999. Less than two weeks after the sale of the 70th home run ball, Philip Ozersky attended the annual dinner of the St. Louis chapter of the Baseball Writers Association of America, as a guest of the Cardinals. Pope John Paul II was due in town the next day, Mark McGwire was to be honored by the writers as baseball's Man of the Year, but Ozersky was very much the man of the hour.

One of the highlights of Ozersky's evening, other than the chance to bash elbows with childhood heroes like Lou Brock and Bob Gibson, came at what once might have seemed a steep price. NBC sportscaster Bob Costas auctioned a caricature of McGwire on horseback, donated by a local cartoonist, with the proceeds to benefit the slugger's charitable foundation, and various charities designated by the writers.

When the bidding slowed at $2,500, McGwire took the microphone from Costas and offered to sign the picture with a personalized message to the winning bidder. "This is worth more than the ball," McGwire joked. "I touched this."

Ozersky had thought about bidding on the item, as a gesture to the people in the Cardinals office who had been kind enough to invite him to the event in the first place, and as a public show of his good intentions, and now he thought about it some more. He kept coming back to the fact that he still hadn't met McGwire. He'd been in the same room with him, but they'd never actually spoken. McGwire knew who he was—Ozersky's brother Alan had heard a second-hand version of a conversation McGwire reportedly had with a mutual acquaintance in California—but Ozersky was anxious to meet him directly. More than that, he wanted to meet him on neutral turf. After all he'd been through, he couldn't see having to chase down McGwire in a crowded room. He couldn't see introducing himself. It would feel a little like stalking, he thought. He didn't want to come across as a desperate fan.

Ozersky bid on the picture, at $3,000, but the bidding accelerated with McGwire's pledge to sign the item. Costas called out the bids in $500 increments, and Ozersky raised his hand every now and then. His head was clouded in the same kind of way he imagined the people at the Guernsey's auction had been clouded in their thinking. He'd wondered what it would be like, to bid on an item without any real regard for the money involved, to decide to buy something at a certain price and find yourself bidding ten times that amount, and now he knew.

Throughout the evening, Ozersky'd had some time to visit with the people at his table, and they were encouraging him in his bidding, egging him on. They knew his story. They knew how high he could go. Happily, for the charities involved, the other bidders had deep pockets as well (they turned out to be the wives of the Cardinals owners), and when the bidding stopped Ozersky held the winning offer—at $11,000. He stood to a round of applause, but people in the far reaches of the banquet room had no idea who he was. As he made his way to the dais, Ozersky heard Costas joke about how it was too bad Philip

Ozersky wasn't on hand to drive the price even higher. A few of the sportswriters in attendance had by this time recognized Ozersky as the buyer, and before Ozersky could reach the podium the banquet room buzzed with his name.

At this point, most of the two thousand fans, sportswriters, and Cardinals dignitaries in attendance had all made the connection, and most stood to acknowledge the young man's generosity. Lou Brock himself (the greatest base stealer of all time, Ozersky didn't care what Rickey Henderson had to say about it) crossed the room to shake Ozersky's hand and thank him for his largesse, but for the moment the guy who used to own Mark McGwire's 70th home run ball had only one legend in his sights.

Ozersky reached for McGwire's hand, and when he shook it, he felt smaller than he had in his adult life. The man was positively enormous, Ozersky remembered thinking. Just huge. Fe-fi-fo-fum huge, and Ozersky couldn't shake feeling like Jack. They small talked, and it was as if the entire off-season had melted away. It was September 27 once more, and they were back in the Cardinals clubhouse, and Ozersky was swapping his story of how he came to grab the ball for one of McGwire's, of how he came to hit it. They were in this thing together, connected by a single baseball.

After a while, McGwire whispered to Ozersky, off mike. He wanted to know if he wanted the picture signed to Philip or to Phil. "How do you spell Philip?" he asked, wanting to know the number of *l*s in his name, wanting to get it right for the caricature. And, as long as he was making sure, he asked, "How do you spell catch?"

Ozersky spelled everything out for him, and as McGwire held the signed caricature up for all to see ("To

Philip, Great Catch!"), it occurred to Ozersky how simple this moment was. How human. He'd built it up in his head, to where the idea of meeting McGwire was almost too big to grasp. It was all going to be so very much larger than life, but now that it was here he realized it wasn't larger than life at all. It was exactly the right size.

File this under Clash of the Icons.

The power of Mark McGwire's appeal in St. Louis earned him an audience with Pope John Paul II, outside the Kiel Center sports arena, home of the St. Louis Blues National Hockey League team. The Pope was scheduled to address twenty thousand area youngsters on Tuesday afternoon, January 26, in what was billed as a "Light of the World" youth rally. The event was planned as a centerpiece of the pontiff's thirty-hour tour of the city. He stopped for a brief visit with McGwire on the way in. McGwire, a Catholic, kissed the Pope on his right hand.

At the event—a strobe-lit pep-rally sort of affair, notable for the enthusiastic waving of what appeared to be twenty thousand yellow scarves—the Pope demonstrated his ability to work any room and invoked the local sports hero to make his point. He urged the young people in attendance to set their minds on clear paths, to train for their lives as Catholics the way the home run kings Mark McGwire and Sammy Sosa might train for the coming baseball season, or for the World Series. Following Christ was a vocation, he said, a calling, not unlike baseball.

Earlier in the day, during a twenty-minute meeting between the Pope and President Bill Clinton at Lambert-St. Louis International Airport, *New York Times* reporter James Bennet noticed a sectioned-off area near the function room where the summit had been arranged. "If there was any doubt," Bennet wrote in his account the next morning, "that by virtue of his position Mr. Clinton occupied as lofty a plane as the Pope today—or that the Pope, by virtue of being human, has some of the same needs as Mr. Clinton—it was erased by the sign marking a rest room near their meeting room." The sign read, PRESIDENT OR HOLY FATHER ONLY.

Mark McGwire was across town at the time of this particular meeting, but the question was raised: If he had to go, would they let him use the facilities?

January 28, 1999. Ettinger again pressed for a selling bonus, this time suggesting to Freedland he might hold up payment on Ozersky's share of the proceeds of the Aaron ball, which he indicated had not yet sold. Separately, Barnes had learned from Richard Arndt's attorney that a private sale had been concluded at $650,000, through Guernsey's, with Aaron agreeing to take 25 percent for his "Chasing the Dream" foundation, instead of the original 42.5 percent. The new math allowed Arndt to collect the same $464,000 he would have seen had the ball met its $850,000 reserve price on January 12.

It's possible, Ettinger said, that since the ball did not sell at auction, Guernsey's agreement to split its proceeds down the middle might be considered void. After all, the 50-50 deal only covered the Mantle and Aaron balls if they sold at the auction, and there was industry precedent to support the position that a post-auction sale would be subject to different terms.

In most cases, an auction house retains the right to sell certain items for a period of time beyond a scheduled auction—say, thirty or sixty days—and Ozersky's advisers believed their client was entitled to his 50 percent share under these extended terms. At $650,000, Guernsey's 15 percent buyer's premium and reduced-rate 5 percent sellers' commission came to $130,000, which left Ozersky entitled to $65,000.

And yet here was Arlan Ettinger, seeking his $35,000 selling bonus and arguing that Ozersky's $65,000 Aaron payment was by no means assured.

February 1, 1999. At 10:04 A.M. eastern standard time, a bank transfer in the amount of $2.7 million was wired from a Guernsey's account at a Manhattan branch of Marine Midland Bank to a St. Louis branch of Northern Trust Bank.

At 2:23 P.M. eastern time, Ozersky's bank in St. Louis was in receipt of funds, although he was not notified of the transaction until approximately six o'clock that evening, by cellular phone, as he was leaving the genome lab on the Washington University campus. He was dressed casually, in a pair of corduroy pants and pullover fleece top. On his feet, he wore socks and a pair of open-toed Birkenstock sandals. He felt, he said, "anti-climactically rich."

Before he left, he notified his supervisors that he would be taking a reduced role at the lab, going forward. He was still committed to his work, he said, and to the genome project, but he didn't want his uncertain schedule to get in the way of the lab's overall productivity. He stepped down from his position as assistant coordinator of the finishing lab and vowed to continue his work as a finisher as soon as possible. This way, at least, his mounting absences wouldn't slow any of his colleagues, and he could simply resume isolated work on his own assignments when his ball-related life settled down.

Later, he drove to his parents' house to retrieve a three-page fax transmission from Ettinger, who had now thought to make his case for a selling bonus in writing. In the letter, which sounded to Ozersky like a tear-soaked confession, Ettinger outlined some of his expenses in mounting the sale and his frustrations at not being able to fully participate through his usual commission schedule. He was still looking for what Ozersky couldn't shake thinking was a $35,000 gratuity. Ettinger said that in offering to waive his seller's fee, he actually forgot about the reduced buyer's premium on sales over $1 million. He referred Ozersky to an urgent phone call made to Michael Freedland, when it appeared Ozersky would pull out of the sale and accept the one-year lease deal from Florida businessman Edd Helms, that resulted in Ettinger agreeing to waive his seller's commission entirely. "Please understand," he wrote, "that the call was made not from my office, where I would have had access to notes regarding earlier negotiations, but rather the call was made on a pay phone in a somewhat dingy, noisy, smoke-filled bar near our warehouse."

Ozersky called Freedland after he'd read the letter. "Can you believe this guy?" he said.

February 3, 1999. Ozersky and Abbott arrived in Amsterdam for an appearance on a television program called *Gekkenhuis!*—or *Crazy House!* The show, a production of Joop van den Ende, seemed to Ozersky to be a Dutch version of *That's Incredible!* wherein guests shared their amazing stories for the cameras.

Joining Ozersky on the program were a woman with Double H breasts, another woman who had undergone twenty-five plastic surgeries, and an overweight woman who owned and operated a lingerie store for other overweight women.

For his trouble, Ozersky received round-trip airfare for two, hotel accommodations, and two bottles of wine.

February 8, 1999. Several dozen reporters gathered at the Plaza Hotel in New York for a press conference to announce Todd McFarlane as the owner of the 70th home run ball, and eight other record baseballs from the 1998 season. Bagels and coffee were served.

McFarlane, the thirty-seven-year-old comic book publisher and toy manufacturer, might have stepped forward sooner, but he was in Sarasota, Florida until the night before, playing baseball in the Baltimore Orioles fantasy camp, on a team coached by former Orioles catcher Andy Etchebarren. He intended to leave early, but his team made the camp championship, and he couldn't miss out on a thing like that, not even for a thing like this.

"I don't want to keep these balls hidden," he said, outlining his plans to put the balls on tour. In addition to the 70th home run ball, he also purchased McGwire's 1st, 63rd, 67th, 68th, and 69th home run balls and Sosa's 33rd (representing his 20th home run in the month of June, a record), 61st and 66th. "I don't want them to be mine," he insisted. "I want them to travel, to be out there." He said he had no plans to charge money for fans to view his collection. Instead, his thinking was he could maybe leverage the balls with big league clubs for the chance to take twenty batting practice swings in every major league ballpark. He was kidding, but he was also serious. In describing himself to the skeptical members of the press, he said he was the kind of guy who would toss everything he had for the chance to play center field for a major league baseball team. He called his purchases a mixture of business, charity, and self-indulgence to the nth degree.

The total cost, for all nine balls, including buyer's premiums, was $3,609,800. "I blew my life savings on this," he assured the media. "I blew my wad. I'm not Donald Trump. I don't have a lot of cash, but what I do have, you see in these balls right here." Prior to these purchases, McFarlane said he had a decent collection of sports memorabilia, including the uniform worn by Madonna in the Penny Marshall movie *A League of Their Own*. But nothing approached the McGwire ball, which he kept calling "the big boy." He said he was so excited about the prospect of buying such a sought-after item that he asked his friend Al Simmons, the man for whom he named his *Spawn* character, to videotape the bidding. Now, in addition to the nine baseballs, he also had a badly-framed tape of himself on the telephone, entering his bids.

McFarlane answered questions for about an hour, during which, for a comic book illustrator, he was appropriately animated. He was funny, relaxed, and keenly aware that most people thought he was out of his mind for doing what he did. When one reporter asked where he planned to store the balls, when they weren't on display, and if he was worried about insurance or other safekeeping issues, he answered that he was less concerned about security than his business advisers. "One day," he said, "when nobody's looking, I might even toss one of them around in the backyard." But for the most part, he said, he will have to enjoy the balls from a distance; he won't be able to roll around naked with them or anything cool like that.

What did he think the 70th home run ball would be worth if the record fell during this coming season?

"Well," he declared, "I go from being the idiot that spent three million dollars on the crown jewel of sports memorabilia to the idiot that spent three million dollars on a five-dollar ball. I'm here to tell you that I made the biggest bet in the world that the record won't fall anytime too soon. If it does, I've got nine good months underneath me, but if it gets too close, then again, I saw what Tonya Harding did a few years back. There are options."

When he tried to explain to his wife his pursuit of the 70th home run ball in terms she could understand, McFarlane admitted he was baffled. He found there were no cultural equivalents for women. About the closest he could get, from the women he polled, was Leonardo diCaprio, in shorts, dancing live, in a case. Men and women get silly in different ways, he determined. He imagined a big room, with two crowds of people. Around one case, there'd be a crowd of women, watching Leonardo diCaprio dance. And around the other, there'd be a crowd of men, looking at the home run ball with their mouths open.

He kept referring to his passion for sports as silly, but he was willing to defend himself. "Sports are one of the few things in the world that makes us forget about death, taxes, politics, and all the other garbage that sometimes goes on in our life," he reasoned. "All you know is, he likes Dallas, and you like Philadelphia, and you shut everything else down. All the walls, all the barriers we have as individuals, as humans, go down, and when you talk about sports, it's just sports, and the only arguments you really have are: Was Babe Ruth a better ballplayer than Roger Maris, or Mark McGwire? Was Gordie Howe better than Gretzky? Was Chamberlain better than Michael Jordan? Those are the only arguments you really have, and those are kind of silly. Women don't indulge themselves in those ones. But it just shuts us down and makes us forget the drudgery sometimes that's there, 'cause I read the front page too. We're dealing with our nation's leader, on a subject we shouldn't even be talking about. We should have something else on the front page right now."

The next morning, McFarlane visited radio talk show host Howard Stern, to talk about his purchase and subject himself to some fun at his own expense. Stern, an avowed fan of McFarlane's HBO series *Spawn* and a long-time comic book collector, razzed McFarlane mercilessly for blowing $3 million on a baseball. McFarlane took the criticism with good cheer and justified his purchases gallantly. He even offered Stern and his on-air staff the opportunity to hold some of the record home run balls, to see if maybe the thrill in owning such record-setting items would rub off on them.

At the close of the segment, when Stern's sidekick Robin Quivers asked if McFarlane might be experiencing some kind of buyer's remorse, and if the value of these items had possibly gone down since the night of the auction, the ball's new owner responded as if rehearsed. "No," he insisted. "I think the value just went up. I'm one of the few males in this country who can say 'Howard Stern touched my balls.'"

Don't go telling Gary Summers he doesn't know a good idea when he thinks of one.

Trouble was, he hadn't been able to bring Phil Ozersky

or any of his conservative advisers to his way of thinking. Mark McGwire and his camp wanted no part of his plans, which left Summers deep into the second deck, in terms of the cards he generally kept up his sleeve. His fantasy home run, virtual reality proposal was a big ticket, he felt sure, but he was missing one key element to his proposal: the 70th home run ball. Actually, two: the ball *and* Mark McGwire, but he had every reason to believe one would follow the other.

Summers watched Todd McFarlane on the news and thought, okay, this was a guy he could do business with. This was a guy with a sense of humor. Summers had a sense of humor all his own, and he wanted to appeal to McFarlane's. He wanted to reach out to him in a creative way, so he cribbed some images from the comic book *Mage* and pasted together a storyboard, casting himself as a superhero in pursuit of "baseball's Holy Grail." In place of Mage's scepter, his "Gary Summers" character wielded a baseball bat, and in one panel he referred to the ball as "a piece of American pie." It was, he thought, a clever presentation, and underneath was Summer's pitch: sign on to a marketing plan that now called for as much as $139,960,000 in revenues, and make us both a ton of money.

Summers was given to speaking in tons.

The one downside, far as Summers could tell, was Mc-Farlane might have to give up the ball in the bargain. Or, he might not. It depended on whether the winner of the fantasy home run contest opted to keep the ball as the grand prize, or a tax-free cash payment of $1 to $2 million. Summers was still tinkering with the formula. He estimated there was a 90 percent chance McFarlane could hold onto his ball, but the possibility existed that it would have to be given away in the promotion.

Other than that, though, Summers couldn't think of one reason why the guy wouldn't go along with his plans. Not one.

During the first weeks of February, as pitchers and catchers reported to the St. Louis Cardinals spring training complex in Jupiter, Florida, the talk centered on Mark McGwire. The sideline commentary bounced back and forth between here-we-go-again complacency and still-having-trouble-believing-it incredulity, while underneath the talk was an affirmation that life and baseball can't help but go on, even in the heady aftermath of legendary accomplishments.

It is a cyclical thing, our national game. Observers noted that in no other sport do fans and participants begin each season so thoroughly anew. What was once history making and breathtaking quickly becomes a part of baseball's rich quilt, and in the stitching together of what has come before to what will happen next there exists the broadest of possibilities. Anything can happen— and, in time, most everything does. A hulking kid from Pomona, California can burst onto the scene with 49 home runs in his rookie year and build a career out of threatening the single-season home run mark before smashing it into small pieces. An unassuming research scientist can hurl his body atop a record-setting home run ball and come away with nearly $3 million for his trouble. An ace pitcher can land a $105 million contract and tilt the balance of power to where small-market teams no longer weigh in on the same scale as big market clubs, while a first-year player making the league minimum can mean the difference in a pennant run. Immortals will prove mortal, unlikely heroes will reach immortality, and the game will continue.

Baseball occupies unique territory. It is a game hasped not at all by time, and hardly at all by space, and yet it has rooted itself in the cultural firmament in a fixed, timeless manner that belies its own boundaries. It is, for the most part, as it will ever be (at least for the run of the current labor agreement), no matter how many pinky-ringed speculators turn out to make a market in its tokens.

In time, the tokens themselves—the game-used bats and balls and presumably washed undershirts—will carry more meaning when we rub up against them firsthand, when the memories they hold are ours and not someone else's. In time, Philip Ozersky's home run ball will look different to us than Todd McFarlane's, no matter what the authenticators say. In time, we will remember the man who caught it ahead of the man who bought it, because there are some things even $3.005 million cannot buy.

February 15, 1999. Philip Ozersky finally sat down with his sister Sharon and his brother-in-law, Brian Button, to map a plan for his charitable foundation.

Ozersky was still expecting to donate heavily to the Leukemia Society and to the American Cancer Society—$70,000 seemed an appropriately round number for each—and he was working with Mike Barnes to develop an ongoing giving plan with Cardinals Care. Right now, they were considering a home run derby sort of donation, through which Ozersky might contribute $100 for every 1999 Cardinals home run, and maybe $700 for every McGwire home run hit at home. They'd call it "The Phil

Ozersky Challenge," or something. By any name, it was a good way to have some fun with it, and to remind people of McGwire's singular accomplishment and what it continues to mean, although when they presented the idea to Ed Lewis, the director of Cardinals Care, it was received with only mild enthusiasm.

According to Lewis, Cardinals manager Tony LaRussa wasn't thrilled with the notion of a charitable donation keyed to home run output, because it might negatively impact on the team's performance. Already, the Starbucks corporation had announced a plan to fund a local literacy program through McGwire's home run totals, and LaRussa worried the concept would place the player's focus on hitting home runs instead of winning ball games. A true Cardinals fan, he reportedly suggested to Lewis, would come up with some kind of program tied to total team victories.

Barnes and Ozersky thought this was something they could work with, but they still wanted to somehow connect it to the number 70. Maybe $100 for every Cardinals win up to a season total of 70, and $1,000 for every victory thereafter. Or, $200 for the first 70, and $2,000 after that. They wanted a formula that would yield something near a $50,000 annual contribution, because Ozersky didn't want to tap himself out in just one season of giving. He wanted to keep connected to the Cardinals and to Cardinals Care for as long as he could. He wanted people to remember McGwire's record as having helped the community.

But mostly, he wanted to get his charitable foundation off the ground, and as he sat with his sister and brother-in-law, he thought through ways to combine his love of sports with Mark McGwire's public dedication to disadvantaged and abused children. All along, Sharon Button had been telling her brother he should conduct his post-ball life in ways that would make McGwire proud, and here he was being faced with his first sustained opportunity to do so.

A summer camp for kids, they decided, was the way to go. It was something Ozersky had been thinking about since the very first day, when he realized the kind of money the sale of his ball might bring. The emphasis would be on team sports, possibly with the interaction of professional athletes, and certainly with the involvement of counselors and educators specializing in working with abused children. They could start small and grow, from a single week the first summer to longer sessions in subsequent years. At some point, Ozersky thought, it would be nice to expand to overnight sessions.

He'd place his efforts under the umbrella of something called The 70 Foundation, or A Home Run for Kids Foundation. He'd figure out what to call it later, but he'd start with a $300,000 contribution, and then develop ways to solicit corporate sponsorship, investment, and community participation. It was the kind of thing that could grow to a full-time job, if he did it right. He could run it with Sharon and Brian. It would be his legacy, at least as far as catching Mark McGwire's 70th home run ball was concerned.

As Ozersky set his thoughts to paper, he realized this was the greater good he was talking about, ever since the season ended. He always felt he would recognize it, when he came across it, and here it was. This was what that ball could do for the children of St. Louis. This was what the ball could do for him. This was the reason it landed in his hands, and not in someone else's

Acknowledgments

Several people had a hand in the building of this book, and rate a mention here. Tom Rock, of Long Island's *Newsday*, offered invaluable research assistance and background reporting; his extra efforts and initiatives are reflected throughout the final manuscript.

Of the hundred or so individuals who graciously submitted to interviews, none were more patient or insightful than Kevin Hallinan, Ed Petersen, Linda Pantell, Ruben Puente, and Brian O'Gara of Major League Baseball; National League umpire Richard Rieker; Eric Moriarty of eBay; Miles Standish of Professional Sports Authenticators; Bill Mastro of Mastro Fine Sports Auctions; Larry Shire; Gary Summers; Edd Helms; Jeff Becket; Richard Thomas; Amanda Abbott; Rich Severino and Ron Fiala of the St. Louis Police Department; Bill De Witt III, Tony LaRussa, Buddy Bates, Kurt Schlogl, and Kevin Corbin of the St. Louis Cardinals; Sammy Sosa of the Chicago Cubs; Jack Buck of KMOX-Radio; Aaron Boutwell, Steve Johnson, Mike Cunningham, and Scott Smith of Rawlings; Amye Austin of Guernsey's; and Jeff Idelson of the National Baseball Hall of Fame.

Thanks are also due the record home run ball holders, who generously shared their time, their good fortune, and their unique perspectives: John Grass, Kerry Woodson, Heath Wiseman, Doug Singer, Albert Chapa, Vern Kuhlemeier, and Richard Arndt. Also, to Todd McFarlane and Irwin Sternberg, for a chimerical end to an already improbable tale.

On the publishing side, Wendy Wolf of Viking deserves

a thousand nods for identifying the germ of an idea before it had a chance to spread, and Dan Strone of the William Morris Agency gets 10 percent of these for spreading it just the same; out of this batch, Eric Zohn, also of William Morris, merits at least a couple nods for his key counsel.

At home, the author's wife, Leslie, and three children, Jake, Hana, and Rosie, are owed whole bunches of the time and attention it took for the writing, reporting, and detail-sweating of these pages. Howard Dorman, John Marx, Lee Rimsky, Stephen Latzman, Lee Schreiber, and Jonathan Paisner were ever available to discuss the stories surrounding the sale of Mark McGwire's 70th home run ball, and in some cases, to read portions of the manuscript with care and enthusiasm.

Michael Freedland of the Law Offices of David Krathen, Arlan Ettinger of Guernsey's, and Mike Barnes of Creative Properties Management Group are all deserving of special notice. Their commitment, candor, and inside understanding of the events portrayed herein are everywhere apparent, and endlessly appreciated.

Mostly, though, the author wishes to thank Philip Ozersky, of Washington University's Human Genome Lab, and his own distinct place in baseball history. The book could not have been written without his enormous help, his high-minded spirit, and boundless good cheer, and the great leap of faith that the events of his recent life might stand as a story for our time.

Daniel Paisner
March 1999